ON/OFF
The
BEATEN PATH

The Road Poems

RD Armstrong

© 2008 by RD Armstrong
ISBN 978-1-929878-99-4
All rights reserved.

No part of this book can be reproduced without written permission except in the case of brief quotation in critical essays or review.

Acknowledgments: **A Journey up the Coast** originally appeared as Little Red Book #11 (Lummox Press); **On/Off the Beaten Path** originally appeared as Little Red Book #27 and **RoadKill** was originally published by 12 Gauge Press.

Illustrations and photos by Raindog, unless otherwise noted.

Printed by CreateSpace.com

TABLE OF CONCEPTS

Alive in the Breath *by Todd Moore* 4

A Journey up the Coast 7

On/Off the Beaten Path 32

Roadkill 62

ALIVE IN THE BREATH

Todd Moore

All journeys that lead out also go in. And while the outward journey is filled with geographical splendor and all kinds of surprises, it's the inward journey we long for most because the inward journey is the richest one of all.

Years ago I recall reading A JOURNEY UP THE COAST, ON/OFF THE BEATEN PATH, and ROADKILL. I read each book as it came out in 1999, then in 2000, and finally in 2002. Taken separately, each of these books is both a wide angled view of the west coast and southwest and an intimate look at the narrator. However, if you see these books as travel accounts, then you are seriously mistaken. They are travel books only if you also believe that SONG OF MYSELF and ON THE ROAD also fall into the same category.

Taken as a trilogy JOURNEY, ON/OFF, and ROADKILL form a kind of late twentieth century early twenty first century attempt to recover, recapture, or reinvent a part of america. Also, taken together these three books become a long poem about the rediscovery of america. And, the rediscovery of the self. Beginning with JOURNEY, there is that starting out, that overwhelming desire to get the hell outta Dodge, to BE somewhere else as long as it isn't home. And, as is the case with any "journey out" poem you begin with where you are and you talk about what you see as you leave. The old world is best seen in your rear view mirror. That's the past. In all likelihood, in a week or two you will have to return to that place you are leaving behind. But for the moment, you are existentially and totally free. You have nothing to look forward to except the surprise of where the road will lead and the feeling that you are open to the world.

All three poems begin this way or as a variation of the old "bon voyage." The towns named and renamed along the way, the description of trees and terrain, the lists of friends and memories aren't included as part of the travelese lingo. All of this is there because it's Raindog's attempt to reinvent the west coast and the southwest. Which is also a metaphor for reinventing america. Reinventing and rediscovering. Raindog has somehow become a kind of twenty first century conquistador, minus the horse and the armor, complete with an ironic sense of humor, and the knowledge that the world is no longer as he knew it when he was sixteen or twenty six or thirty six but he knows in his dreams and in his guts that if he can just get out THERE again, if he can drive along the sheer cliffs, the sheetmetal patinaed sea once more then some form of america is still there, still waiting to be seen by a latterday conquistador who will actually conquer nothing but will in some difficult to explain way still be alive in the midst and the breath of the poem and the land.

The only reason I know something about this kind of travel is because I have been there. Along with recover, recapture, and reinvent there is also redemption. Anyone who has ever been an ONTHEROADER will tell you that there is something profoundly redemptive about jumping into a car and lighting out for the territories. I don't know exactly what it is that is redemptive about driving from Los Angeles to Seattle or from Los Angeles to Albuquerque that will redeem anyone, but I do know that there is something about the wonder of completion and surprise about any journey that takes you both OUT THERE and IN HERE.

Maybe it has something to do with eating a big juicy burger and fries in Flagstaff or maybe it has something to do with drinking a glass of O'Doul's and talking about poetry in Vesuvio's or maybe it has something to do with ordering the huevos rancheros at Harry's Roadhouse Café in Santa Fe. It isn't just that but it's the adventure of that and maybe meeting somebody you haven't seen in years there or maybe it's meeting someone you've always wanted to meet and this is finally the chance or maybe it's just the fact that you can walk from Vesuvio's across the alley to City Lights Bookstore or drive from Harry's to the plaza in Santa Fe and talk about the latest book out by John Macker or Kell Robertson or Leonard Cirino. The small anticipations also bring on the larger expectations and finally the dreams of an america you have never seen before but you damn well know is STILL out there and it's somehow waiting just for you.

These anticipations and expectations dominate the first two books. You can find them on practically every page in both small and large ways. However, the seismic shift occurs in ROADKILL when Raindog first hears about 9/11. He both hears about it and watches it take place on television and this event changes the whole mood of this third journey out. Now, more than ever this becomes for Raindog really more of a journey in, a journey into his psychic interior and a questioning of his identity as an american, as well as a poet.

Events like the sinking of the Titanic, Pearl Harbor, the Tet Offensive, and 9/11 leave us all profoundly disturbed and somehow displaced as well. The irony is that any journey is, all by itself, a kind of displacement. Which means that Raindog was doubly displaced when he received the news about the destruction of the World Trade Center.

All journeys out are in some ways tests of our psychic confidence and our physical vulnerabilities. None of us ever anticipate terrible things happening while we are away. I am certain that those who boarded the Titanic only looked forward to the best of voyages, the vistas of a huge ocean, the promise of great talk, and the anticipation of wonderful meals. If you subtract the word Titanic, this is really what Raindog had been looking forward to. When you drive along the Pacific Ocean you can't help but fall in love with that wide expanse of water. And, you can't help but wonder what good things lay in store for you at the end of the highway you are driving along.

In that last part of ROADKILL, Raindog still names and renames cities and towns, still recalls memories of things he had seen before, still recalls old friends and interesting times, but there is a slight change in the ways that he sees things, people, and ultimately his idea of america. Imagine if Kerouac had been writing ON THE ROAD while he was driving up the coast of California. Only instead of the early 50s it's September, 2001. This, naturally is only speculation, but wouldn't it have been interesting if in the midst of writing ON THE ROAD, something as disastrous as 9/11 had occurred. Now, you can probably understand that existential shift in tone that you can see and hear in ROADKILL. It really doesn't matter whether or not Raindog was actually writing this book while he was on the road before, during, and after 9/11. But what it does mean is that the event impacted Raindog's ways of seeing things. It does mean, that whatever Raindog had discovered in the first two books of this trilogy, in ROADKILL he actually discovered his and america's real mortality.

Of all the poetry that Raindog has written, this trilogy is easily his masterwork. All three books belong together and form a larger long poem. When I say long poem I am talking about a work which signals its ambition. Raindog's trilogy is as ambitious a work as John Macker's ADVENTURES IN THE GUNTRADE, Tony Moffeit's BLUES FOR BILLY THE KID, Kell Robertson's A HORSE CALLED DESPERATION, Mark Weber's PLAIN OLD BOOGIE LONG DIVISION, S. A. Griffin's NUMBSKULL SUTRA, and Ron Androla's POET HEAD. What all of these books have in common is that they are outsized long poems or poem sequences and they are all hybrids which incorporate elements of the novel, the memoir, the confession, and the dream. And, they all come from a generation of poets who have been loosely referred to as outlaws.

Raindog's trilogy is not just a longing to recover or reinvent his version of america. it's his attempt to re-envision what he knows of himself and this country. And, it is also his desire to somehow, by writing this trilogy, to heal it and himself.

A JOURNEY UP THE COAST

Introduction

  I am of the generation whose identity was firmly defined by the lures and mysteries of THE ROAD. Nothing is quite as exciting, to me, as the steady whine of the road beneath the tires of my car / truck as I head out of L.A. on my way up Route One or Highway 101 or even the dull repetition of Interstate Five as it careens through the brown-ness of the western San Joaquin Valley.

  My memory of road trips past is tied to vehicles past, as if a particular car or truck can act as a marker along memory lane. The road is so intrinsically interwoven into my history, that I often can't recall the person I was involved with at the time, but I can remember with ease the vehicle I was driving and the many adventures that I had whilst in said vehicle.

  Unfortunately, I took a slight detour during the nineties, distracted by women of various makes & models... But, realizing my error have once again sought the easy comfort of a good travelin' tape, some new sunglasses, a full tank of gas and an inclination for a change of scenery. Just me and a million other drivers... Move over road-ragers, I've got Tom Waits on the stereo and I'm headin' out. See you in two weeks.

  This particular two weeks had an actual itinerary that involved visiting old friends, meeting new ones and doing a little poetic business on the side. No risk of boredom here!

  This poem is based on a diary that I kept. I had originally planned to merely transcribe the diary into book format but ended up "translating/ interpreting" it into the following poem.

RD Armstrong

A Journey up the Coast

In Memory of John Carroll

SANTA CRUZ

Crisp morning Santa
Cruz   5 a.m.
Left Long Beach
10 a.m. yesterday
drove up 101 "just 4

A Journey up the Coast

Old times sake" —
Not much old times left
on 101 except the
rough and tumble
rural areas which
will probably never change
until they are gobbled
up by "progress"
Noticed said progress
outside San Luis Obispo
where, as a lad, I got
stuck hitch-hiking back
to L.A. late one starry night
in spring of '72 (no car)
and had to hike —
no hitching at 3 a.m. —
from San Luis to the sea   10 miles
Took all night but
I was young and determined.
(I didn't know any damned better).
Area is all built up now
was empty space
land and trees.

Stayed with poet Will Taylor, jr.
and girlfriend and cat and bird
in Santa Cruz.   A likable
young man with a
common love of Buk
and the poem
the honest
crisp line.

Santa Cruz reeks of the
almighty "vibe". JS warned me
about it & now I've seen
it walked among it   even
sat down and drank with it.
Just another town in
NoCal. Thank god Will and
co. are good people
good enough to put up a
stranger for the night
(something that was promised

A Journey up the Coast

but proved to be a rarity
later in the trip)
good enough to put up with
all my stories and   "old
man wisdom"

Taylor: Santa Cruz
via   Bakersfield
"by a fluke"
refers to me as his
"publisher" and accords me
a respect that is foreign,
yet familiar — a nostalgic
memory of past lives —

My skills as a publisher
are somewhat dubious
I am unaccustomed to
this new title and the
ensuing acclaim.

I met Will at "LOGOS"
a used/new bookstore in the
good vibing heart of Santa Cruz
Unlike most independent (used)
bookstores   this one
thrives   centrally located in
this college town of young/old
readers. I know I'm not in L.
A. anymore where the cry
for "New!" never ceases.

Driving up 101
found myself drifting
into the memory lane on
more than one
occasion.
Many treks up and
down this highway —
this stretch of road
in the fine company
of the comrades of
youth —
friends and lovers

A Journey up the Coast

companions of those daze
so many years / miles ago
and now I fly solo
(so low).
Funny how certain landscape
features trigger certain
memories
like dreams re-activated
by the piano roll of
time
the
subconscious mind tips open
the dusty old photo album
and out tumbles pictures
from another time —
Karen and her '58 Chevy
four door   bruising tank of a car
riding north through Paso Robles
in the heat of that summer
101 a two-lane country road
in those days   Karen long gone
now.
Thought of her much
this first time on 101
in a dozen years easy.
Look forward to the sad dumb beauty of
these memories as trip unfolds
after house uncurls itself and
the coffee pot is empty.

ROUTE ONE

Two lanes winding
out of desolate coast
lined with sheer cliffs
flat gray drops
into sheetmetal patina sea
cliffs topped with scrub
and bush and wild grasses
wildly rioting at roadside
or freshly mowed and baled
like a KS wheatfield.
Little towns of Davenport
Pescadero, Half Moon

A Journey up the Coast

        Maltera and Venice Beach
        "Where's the sunglasses?"
        Even San Pedro (park)
        "Am I going south or north?"
        Pass a gutted and wind-blasted
        concrete shell of a house —
        it has no access
        no explanation
        just stands on the
        weathered pedestal of sandstone
        perched on top of a hill
        over-looking Half Moon Bay.
        This stretch
        winding
        up to the outskirts
        of SanFran's suburbs
        leads a caravan
        away from the isolation
        of the rugged coastline
        and into Daly City's "little
        boxes" made of ticky-tack
        once a novelty
        now the common
        denominator.
        Bumper to bumper
        on Saturday a.m.?
        Four day weekend   oh yeah   forgot.
        Every motherfather is out
        last minute errands or
        leaving to be with friends
        for the "red glare" that
        no Mureen can cure.
        All these important people —
        as Mike Jensen puts it —
        must reach their
        destination before the
        mass of us   must push
        and claw their way
        every mile wearing on
        them like a D-Day marine.

        It's everywhere
        this insistence
        this assertion

A Journey up the Coast

this <u>I</u>
Not just in evil ol' L.A.
Do I risk personal injury
if I point this out?

Climbing away
from the coast into
gray skies   one   reaches
     the sky   line   and
skirts
            the clouds
with the
rural landscape: straw blond and flattened dull green
trees   the beauty of shades of gray

Suddenly a bend reveals
a herd of suburbia as
frightening and sudden
as a herd of pastel buffalo sweeping
across the hills of South SanFran
dividing into the upper
meadows of Daly City and
the lower industrial flats
of the Cow Palace and SFO.
SanFran lays spread out
before me like a
blanket spread out
over bumpy ground
ready for a July Four picnic
that great American icon
of leisure time   and   success.

ONE OH ONE

Then
it's the rush
to merge
the mad race
of the city.
Sudden and
surprising
The City
(old hippie name)

A Journey up the Coast

rises up
through cracked
concrete —
as if by magic —
and compels
me to face it
on its terms
play by
its rules.
But is this really
SanFran or just
more development?
Could be part of L.A.   easy
Then the towers rising
out of trees as green as
the eyes of envy
the reddish-orange towers
of the "Golden Gate"
a visual password
as familiar as Hewell
Houser confirms
that this is
definitely
The City.

SAN RAFAEL

My brother lives
with two dogs in the hill
country above San Rafael.
We have cable
so we can drown out
the sound of banjoes —
though moonshine flows
like water this weekend.
On his turf
his rules dictate
the transition from
Angelino to Bay-head.
It's a tough regimen
6 a.m.
coffee and Wimbleton
the tennis rackets
beating like insects

A Journey up the Coast

oh the agony
oh the feats of glory
oh the sporting life.
My brother is more mature
though younger than I
More responsible and
focused on working hard   frugal
more conservative   from working hard
"nose to the stone"
without relenting   'til you drop
One of those hard tack guys
with rough hands   you know
tough as nails.   Callused
not hard-hearted though.
His dogs will tell you.
Kodiak and Alexi
big dogs in search of adventure
greeting the day with big
wet kisses and wrestling
for leather "chews"
So I know he's no hard
sombitch   he'd say
just realistic.

I plan to go to Berkeley
to meet Frank Moore
for jam session workout
blowing the notes —
both in style and attempted
technique —   with Marshall
on Frank's Internet radio show.
But traditions loom
and we must submit
to pre-fireworks 4th of July
bar-b-que before I
make my way to
Gillman Street blow-out.

Ill at ease with strangers
I begin to wonder how
I'll fair with the rest of my
SanFran itinerary.
Figure to meet with poets
A.D. Winans   Marie Kazalia   Natalie Y

A Journey up the Coast

    and introduce NoCal to
    Lummox and LRB
    Raindog and THE POEM.
    But food is plentiful
    hosts welcome this stranger
    and soon tales of adventures past
    fill the air as these men of industry
    recall the wild daze of youth.
    My brother
    the worker ant
    celebrates his rest while I
    his vacationing grasshopper prepares
    for another weird moment
    to be added to the charmbracelet of
    dim memories.
    Making my way out of
    the party hoping
    my bro gets home okay
    I head down suburban streets lined
    with trees   neatly manicured houses
    El Cerritosuccessful families
    living the   American dream
    in this year   of 1999   the last year
    of this century.
    Contemplating this transition
    I land at Frank's house
    at 9:15 p.m. unsure of what will
    come next.   I will not be
    disappointed.

    Frank Moore
    that amazing guy
    with MS
    He's pretty much paralyzed
    with marginal use of arms
    and legs   can't talk
    wheelchair bound   just another
    drooling maniac   but
    brother
    what a mind! So intelligent
    and creative
    he's built an empire in the shadow
    of the BART overpass off Gilman
    with his wife   Linda   and Mikee Lebash

carved it out of the wild
and woolly wilderness of the
SanFran/Bay area avant
garde art scene.
His website at www.eroplay.com
operates its own radio station
and it was on this that I
poured my sad little tale out.
Frank would be just another nutjob
in a world already overcrowded
with nutjobs were it not
for the earnest manner
that he approaches his various
projects: teaching   healing   performance
        his faith is unshakable
        as it must be
        since many do not understand
        what it is that he does
It is kooky/ weird/ nutty/ profane
you either love it/ him or you hate it.
I love it/ him.
Frank   Marshall   and I
went at it hammer and tong
for an hour or so
Frank pounding on the piano
coaxing delicate arpeggios out
between "power" chords
Marshall attacked an electric three stringed bass
and a "white noise" generator
while I noodled around on my Casio
digital horn and tone generator.
As comments came in from Japan and
other countries and bombs
exploded in the 'hood around us
we bent down to pick up
the treasures of "found sound"
a trance-like combination
of sound and space
I couldn't know that the sadness
that fills each waking moment
would be so universally accepted
by people I never met.
Such is the blessing of Frank's presence.
He is very fortunate to have

A Journey up the Coast

two people so dedicated to him.
It is heart-wrenching and
at the same time   wondrous
to watch him spelling out words
with his head pointer moving arduously
across the wordboard
his wife translating for him.
Though Frank is about my age
his world is not as easily
maintained
his disease pulls him
down
        down
              down
a little more each day.
It can't be easy on his
family and friends
But I doubt that Frank
thinks that way.   He's on a mission
to save the world
and he just might do it.   It's not so crazy.

ALAMEDA

VH lives off Oakland
on the island of Alameda.
Once a Naval Base
now it is a multi-cultural Mayberry
where Andy & Opie
visit Floyd the Barber.
VH lives with her cats
and her silences

My heart goes out to
her silences and I want to
touch her and smooth
away the sadness that
settles on the house as dusk
approaches as easy as a cat
falling asleep on the cool
tiles of the kitchen floor.
But, even as we say goodby
even as I want to stay
I cannot say the words that

A Journey up the Coast

will   cause us relief.

So I must go and even though
I've always wanted to stay
and have always gone
I know that our lives must
stay separate   that I must always   go.

VESUVIO'S

Unsure of the parking situation
I arrive in North Beach early —
BoHo Mecca on Columbus Ave
next door to Jackie K Alley
and City Lights Books.
I'm meeting A.D. Winans
at this venerated "watering hole"
at eleven this morning.
Twenty till
I give up and pull into a lot.
"Twenty bucks for two hours."   (!@#!&^%!?)
Five minutes later I grab a spot
around the corner.
By the time I've gotten set
it's almost eleven   "Be there on time" a voice
scolds in my head.
I'm early as it turns out.
Vesuvio's has the feel of a neighborhood
bar yet what a neighborhood!
Decorating the walls news clippings of past glories
SanFran's artist elite gathered here
to celebrate life during and after the
Beat heyday   there's Ginberg
This block has drawn the faithful to its
"wall" —   its "city lights"
for some forty five years
only now hip tourists
are snapping pictures through
the windows hoping to catch the   next Ginsberg.
A few years ago the next Ginsberg
may have driven up Eye Five
with me to this block to read
at a bar in the Mission.

A Journey up the Coast

We three poets from angel city
Jay   Donna   Rain
emerged under gray skies
and hit the Hotel Europa
across the ave and above the Condor
Room   "Where Carol Doda got her start!"
It was perfect
a dreary dump that smelled of
burnt cooking oil and
bad decisions.
I couldn't wait to get back to
home to San Pedro.

Winans shows up
and we begin the process.
I've been in contact with him
for about a year and   in my capacity as publisher
have done two books of the Poem
by him   so we meet at last.
Winans like others of his
age is impatiently waiting
to emerge from the shadows
and be venerated as is his right.
To be a poet of the streets
as was Micheline   true and truly
takes an awful toll
the sacrifices are immense:
no retirement
no health insurance
no savings
always working some angle
or another.
To be a working poet in SanFran
is as close as this as anyone would want.
To live by your wits   — an adventure perhaps
not for everyone
for the young maybe
when it's easier to duck as trouble's
fist comes flying at you.
Older is another story
it gets harder to hide from trouble
without succumbing to the temptation
of searching out easy comfort in someone's
safe haven or under the wing of

their patronage.   Maybe a teaching job
saves you from the scrap heap
or maybe you just find a way
that makes sense   and to hell with them!
Winans has found his way
and is emerging into the light at last
with a shred of dignity
and his manhood in tact
is moving to the beat   groupies in tow
A.D. still has charisma with
the ladies   a fine reward for choosing
the poet's life over the time clock's lure
There is no need to impress me
a good cup of Joe   a decent bed   a good shit
maybe a hug   a kiss   a good tape
and the road whining beneath my tires
this is what fills my cup.
Whininess is used to a little better
I think as I nurse my O'Doul's.
Two hours later
after much good chatting
having passed my "exam"
I head down to Market to meet
"new" poet Marie Kazalia.

BROKEN METER

Near the Civic Center
I park across the street from
my destination   Wild Awakenings
so early I can get a bite & slurp
before Marie shows up.
She recently came to my attention
after subscribing to my mag   Lummox Journal
How many mag publishers visit
their subscribers?   It's the personal touch that
Wows them every time!
Judging by her wariness
it was brave of Marie to meet
with me   Who's she been talking to?
But laughter   and not making a move on her
made the words flow easily.
Soon we were chatting like old friends
with The POEM our common interest.

A Journey up the Coast

Sensing time was running out
I excused myself to leave   What's this?
                                       Stay or Go?
                                       Go?
The Golden Gate was wrapped in cotton candy
tourists with cameras clicking in glee.
I was on my way "home".

STINSON

Ever been there?
Getting there   and back
is two thirds the trip.
Redwoods
Scrub Oak
Eucalyptus
Monterey Pine
barren hillside
thick forest
from a sea of boxes
to a sea of slate gray
a row of quaint shops
a row of faded mail boxes
birds wading in red lycra   and cotton
wading birds in snowy white feathers —
no gas station and less than
a quarter tank to go   how far?

WETLANDS

One thing about this area
there's a lot of wet real estate:
wetlands estuaries mudflats lakes
places that   were this L.A.
would be filled in
covered over
lined and striped
metered
and making money.

That's the major difference
and   perhaps
the saving grace.

HARD SELL

Wily Lohman   ala Lee J. Cobb
stares back at me every time
I look in the rear view mirror.
I'm in SanFran to sell books   consign
I am not a salesman
never did the door to door   Amway one day
with any success   Kirby one week
Wily gives me an encouraging
wink at A Different Light on Castro
Wily was coming onto me   The Castro?
I didn't know.
"We prefer a different blah blah blah"
Didn't matter what the theme of the store was
there was always a blah blah blah clause.
Either my books were too straight   or
too weird   or
too boring   or
too hip   or
too obscure   or
too independent   for the independents?
Under   over   sideways round
distributed
wrong channel
right channel
too   "We don't like your kind up here, son."
L.A.
13 stores later
Wily looks disappointed   ashamed
I no longer care by the time
I get into Oakland   Montclair
Espresso at Spasso on College
Then off to meet Cory-Heidi-Alexi   DUDE
Digger Underground Distributing
Enterprise.
Three young locals who will
hawk my wares gladly.
I let them take what they want
glad myself for the delusion
that something is moving
even   if only

A Journey up the Coast

to a third party.

But what a third party!
Encouraging book and music stores
to look at their favorite books and zines
DUDE makes it possible for small
presses like mine to reach a wider audience.
For that   we should all be
grateful and supportive of their efforts.
End of soapbox.

TAXI DRIVER

JB and I go back more than a decade
Knew her in Mar Vista   Venice CA
back in the late eighties
Always liked her as a friend
Would have made a move
but didn't fit proper profile.
After she moved to Oakland
visited her a few times
Been a few years since I last saw her
and family   R and S
Sweet child   delightful
somewhat cranky   bundle of wonder
I do my best to keep her occupied
when I'm not making R crazy
idiot crazy
I bring out the crazy in him   wish it could be
someone else
might not stir up trouble
"I pulled on trouble's braids"   Tom Waits
JB just rolls her eyes   "What can I do?"
Wish he'd find a new shtick
this routine is older than "take my wife please!"
He's the top dog
Alpha male
BMOC
no need to fuck with me   'cept he can
"you lookin' at me?"

A Journey up the Coast

FOR SOFIA (written last day of my stay at JB's)

Particles of light
see how they dance
reflecting
illuminations
a circle of circles
dancing across
the ceiling
waves of light
pushed by hot
summer's breath
that pushes leaves
in undulating trees
that pushes feathers
bending in flight
that pushes blades
of grass on hillsides
and locks of hair
above faces bright
with innocence

that pushes the children
like sheep before
a changing world:
sky of emotion
landscape of wonder
of sorrow
through the horrors
of progress
the glimmerings of joy
a flower surrendering
to the sun
a smile that heals
that kisses away
the bitter taste
of knowledge

the circle of light
radiates outward
bearing a sweet bounty
of innocence
no time is present
the ticking clock

A Journey up the Coast

counts for nothing
heatwaves shimmer
and the breath stops
anticipating the return
of sleep

the day begins
and the children
begin their search

what mysteries
await their curiosity
will they dance
on the wind
or merely wander
through the nightmares
of their parents
creation.

BODEGA (Meditations at Land's End)

Freewheeling through NorCal
going where I please
not always pleased with where I go.
This journey began as a sidetrip
to Sacramento in a heatwave.
Men do questionable things in hot weather.
One hundred seven degrees is
about twenty degrees to hot to
be rational   or intelligent
In the shadow of the state capitol
men shed metaphors
like lizards on a molten stage
and women smoldered in post-feminist-modern-pastiche
barely containing rage at the evils
of the white race   male
Glad to get away
even at eleven p.m.   99 degrees
headed west   Bay area   no place to stay
not caring   just wanting   out of there.

Ended up at the NoTel Motel
on Richmond border
catch a few hours sleep   "Forty Dollar cash!"

A Journey up the Coast

There's porno on the tube
and a fucking mirror
over the bed!   Figures
I'm jerking off to get to sleep
in this fuck fort — solo   FIGURES!
I had such hopes for this trip
here I am a nice congenial guy
selling a few books here and there
not an ax murderer!
Dawn cracked hard
no point in staying too long
Meeting Sis for breakfast in Oakland hills
then I'm at loose ends again what to do?
Eggs and coffee and catching up on
music and other projects
Sis is busy staying away from trouble's braids
I'm lucky to get the time I do.
Eggs are gone and she
must go too   commitments
Bye bye see you in a few more years.

The Stinson loop becomes a ride up the coast
after a failed trip to the Muir Woods not 4th?
No place to park so I head to the one-oh-one
towards Bodega Bay and Jenner on the one
sixteen out of Petaluma.
Held captive by the heat
I mistakenly think that one sixteen
will take me to Sebastapol
thinking Petaluma is Santa Rosa   it's not.
Bodega Bay —
once home to my friend Chris Sauve
dead these two years of an overdose —
is no short haul from Petaluma home to Tom Waits
On the two lane that
cuts through hills to the coast
I slip into an easy rhythm
and thoughts turn to this
road as a metaphor:
How many have gone down this
road never to return?   This is an omen
This lonely path is tough on the solitary traveler
better to make the journey
with a comrade

27

A Journey up the Coast

    someone to share the insights with
    "I'm finally coming into my own"   and no one's here
    someone to confirm the double rainbows
    to witness the close calls.
    Funny
    Most of my trips up this stretch
    have been solo jaunts
    Most of my driving adventures   post sobriety
    have been alone
    There is an uneasy connection to this
    northern coast
    a memory   threadbare after 20 years
    of events along highway
    one sixteen east and the
    Russian River.
    Where I skinny-dipped with Diane
    and made love to Karen
    and was nearly flattened with Carl
    who knew Kris   of Alaska
    and Gary —   ???
    roommates from the Berkeley daze
    some 28 years back in time
    yet with me now as I wind
    through hills as still as dry straw.

    Little towns stubbornly fight with   El Nino
    to stay put
    towns like Monte Rio — Rio Nido — Guernville
    flooded out but still standing
    These memories —
    overflowing the banks   making a mess
    I shake off the cobwebs   time to move on
    Making the big curve that leads
    back to the one-oh-one
    just past Sebastapol   on one-sixteen
    I recall the same vista coming
    back from visiting Carl in Rio Nido
    I was driving the Valiant   '67 Plymouth
    back to Berkeley.
    Same car I was driving when
    I realized that the journey
    between point "A" and "B" was
    as important and sometimes
    even more so.

A Journey up the Coast

Now eating bread & cheese
in the near-silence of the Bodega Headland
I see that the journey to reach this
spot   at this time   on this day
has focused my thoughts
into a meditation.
I am a seeker   a pilgrim
a solitary traveler
searching for an understanding
a peaceful reconciliation
with my self   and my maker.
This not just a road trip —
not just a road trip
but then it never is   is it?

HOMEWARD / ADIOS SANFRAN

Clement Street diner   "Eats"
approximately reminiscent of old
Ed Hopper's painting
three people sitting
in the Clement side window:
A.D. Winans   Natalie Y   Raindog
"lunch" and loose talk
about loose days and loose ways.
My second meeting with AD
joking easy now
as if that easy bond of friendship
had come at last.
Ms. Natalie is sweet and sexy
in that European way
with faint accent of mother Russia
spicing up plain thoughts
gift wrapping the words
making this day as special:
my last day in SanFran.
Outside
we mug for cameras at a bus stop
my point-and-shoot
looking Cro-Magnon next to
AD's flat black 35 mm   Canon?
all streamlined and modern
Goofing with a beer billboard

A Journey up the Coast

appearing to be pre-occupied with booze
(while I'm pre-occupied with sex)
Soon we must make our adieus
Natalie prepares to fly to NY
to read at The Bitter End
AD heads home to organize his papers
Raindog must return to SR and then
it's adios SanFran
exiting the next day at 6:30 a.m.
beating the heat of both day and traffic
I head south on 280 an unfamiliar highway
traveling above Stanford   Mountain View   Menlo Park
and other towns of the lower peninsula
280 joins the 101   already in progress
just outside San Jose
southbound I leave the traffic behind.
Next stop Santa Maria.
Just past the "halfway" mark San Luis Obispo
I pull into Santa Maria to see
my cousin Ruth and hubby DJ.
Lunch and catch-up   "how's...?"
whirlwind visit will have to do
as the road calls to me
I feel the tug of L.A. like some gravitational force
mysterious yearnings to be in
the arms of my town again.
One last stop before
donning the outfit of Angelino in earnest:
the art colony of Ojai
at the corner of the 150 & 33 highways
past orange groves
over hill and dale
dropping into Ojai valley
to visit Sooz   "Stop by on the way home"
mother of Jasper and ex-wife of Peter
former San Pedro resident
artist   jeweler   friend.
Breaking bread
I share the bounties of her world:
fresh fruits and vegetables
the pleasure of fresh sheets
of friendly words
the kindness of fellowship   and the Poem
I am dog-tired and decline a jaccooz

A Journey up the Coast

hitting the hay before midnight   a rarity.

Dawn whispers to me like an impatient child
until I can't ignore it anymore and rise
to recap my journey in the diary.
Sitting on the bed staring out
the window at the changing light
thoughts of lazy idleness slowly trans
form into thoughts of pending obligations:
jobs   rent   bills   deadlines
and I know that I am already home
that the last leg of the trip
is a mere formality
to get my physical self into
position with my mind
with my life.

IMAGINARY SKYLINE

ON / OFF THE BEATEN PATH
(The Book of ON – mostly)

Introduction to THE BOOK OF ON

      On/Off, On/ Off, On/Off...The pattern repeats itself until the pattern becomes rote, until the pattern becomes a statement of fact: irrefutable and undeniable. I had hoped that this poem would shed some light on my parallel (and perilous) journey through the scarred mindscapes of New Mexico. I say parallel since I was reliving a similar trip taken some 17 years earlier, yet in my mind's eye there was no distinction between the two eras, though, in reality I am two distinct individuals...or so I thought.

      The reality is I am not all that different today, than I was 17 years ago, with one possible exception, one that affects my ability to crawl out of bed in the morning and recall what I did the night before. The difference is I'm 16 years sober.

      The significance of that time becomes apparent when I tell you it was the start of the last year of an awful time in my life, a time when I lost touch with just about everything of value to me, including my life.

      Imagine my mixed feelings when I realized that I was glimpsing the shadows of that past on this rather innocent trip to NM. A chance to make a final and lasting peace with the old demons of my squandered youth. To bury the hatchet and let go of my shame as one might release a balloon...bye bye, baby. But the shadow remains just that, a phantom. This past is buried deep, the wound has healed over, the scars, just barely visible to the discerning eye (I?). It will take another pilgrimage to NM to shake loose that cycle of on /off. Possibly more.

So it begins...

On/Off the Beaten Path

PREFACE

Washington DC – 1980

A photograph of a nude woman
seated on the floor next to a
stone sculpture.

A moment in a life captured
with photographic exactitude.
In spite of the sculptor's chisel
the soul of the stone remains
unchanged after twenty years
and the soul of that woman
still haunts the memory.

For Georgia Cox
whose friendship and kind wishes
have lasted far longer than I deserve

Fragments
as if the world is glimpsed
through a broken mirror —
A mosaic of shattered moments
sewn together ala the patchwork
quilt of memory:

At a gas station in Newberry
Springs Regis Philbin drones
while I buy my first tank of gas
outside L.A.
Nearby
a solar collector station
patiently absorbs sunlight
— magical conversion near Barstow
land of maroon hoods and freight yard's clang.
High desert rolls off
into the great beyond
rolling up to the base of
burnt igneous rocks
as if swept by ancient sirocco

On/Off the Beaten Path

    brooms as if (no carpets
    available) ancient sands
    from old Route 66 became
    fill for jagged volcanic arroyos.
    Clusters of rock the color of dried blood
    thrust up through this high desert sandbox
    like broken teeth on an
    upturned jawbone
    as if here, the earth is
    a battered skull or some part
    of a skeletal geology
    exposed
    to weather.
    Magma fingers
    stubbed and broken
    reaching skyward
    surrendering to sun's
    indifferent attention.

LIKE BROKEN TEETH ON AN
UPTURNED JAWBONE . . .

Interstate 40
Modern highway
four lanes
twice the convenience
of the Hillbilly Highway
Ancient Route 66
the once and future link
Chi-town to EL LAY
two lanes of history
two lanes synonymous with the romance of
THE ROAD

Kerouac
On the Road Again
Bobby Troup
Get your kicks on Rte. six six
Wanderlust
See the USA in your Chevrolet
James Dean
Airstream
Motel 6.

Route 66
shadows I-40
two lanes of cracked
asphalt that keeps
coming back to
haunt the memory
as visions of simpler times
return again and again

Route 66
like some prehistoric
tar-encrusted
Loch Ness monster
appearing out of
desert wilderness
to dog the trail
of I-40 and spook
the traveler with nightmares of
less than a quarter of
a tank of gas and
"next services 55 miles"

On/Off the Beaten Path

Route 66
asphalt serpent
snaking from Barstow
to Needles
through Kingman
to Flagstaff
past Gallup
to ABQ and on
to Amarillo
and Oklahoma City beyond
(where 168 chairs wait for no one).
A red line on the map
cutting into the sandy bottom
of this long-dead sea bed
this forsaken geography
of pulverized rock fields
fossilized trees
lava fields and sandstone.
Unchanged.
Timeless except
for the whimsy and folly
of the Land Lord:
man.

A train moves across the
desert like Morse Code –
dots and dashes heading
south towards Amboy
all washed in muted hues of desert
grays and greens.

Needles flashes by like a junkie's promise.
Colorado River cuts a lazy swath
twisting gently towards Baja and
Sea of Cortez.
Crawling uphill towards AZ proper
Ocatillo whips in bloom
Holy Moses Wash
Andy Devine Parkway
Shinarump Avenue
CB World.
Sandstone slab walls
retaining hills older than dirt

Kingman traffic jam session
(twenty cars) – deserted road
suddenly crowded with urgency.
Fractured lava caps
sandstone cliffs
red and stoic as if
Indians wait to charge down
on hapless wagon trains along
Interstate Forty
ala John Ford western epic.

Climbing now, eyeball to eyeball
with red-tailed hawk
and sore-assed snowbirds
migrating north for the summer.
Five thousand feet of
blue sky spreading wide
like smile on mother of
prodigal son
then sudden puff of
single cotton-tail cloud
drifting lazy
across vast and holy blueness.
Williams
Bellemont
McConnico
Yucca
all but forgotten names
of once bustling towns
back when ancient 66 was THE MAIN DRAG
the only game in town.
Now progress dictates:
I-40 will ignore all towns
wherever possible.
Top Rock
Ash Fork (where gas-jock asks me
almost wistfully where I'm a-headin)
Like crosses marking errors in
judgement, highway signs mark passage
and progress towards the ever-onward.
Devil Dog Road
Flagstaff – forty miles
Rest stop – seventeen miles to the Flag
Spotty log entries

On/Off the Beaten Path

as if distracted by something
anxious looks over the shoulder
quick shot to the left
"what was that?"
Nothing is there
nothing visible
But something lurks & lingers
something past – more than
just the taste of PB&J
at 6500 feet —
savoring flavors and
wondering what is playing
tag with my consciousness.

"Arizona Main Street Town"
Founded 1882 – Pop. 65 M
Home of Arizona's highest:
Humphrey's Peak
12,663 feet above sea level
5,663 feet above Flagstaff
Ponderosa Pine trees
Lonesome train horns
woo-whooing from town-center
snow on the ground
like a dirty carpet of freezer-burn ice cream.
Purple beams against
cedar shingles and flag stones
jarring loose a memory of a *'46 Dodge*
3 ton w/
Snub-nosed Cab
and 16 foot bed
Flathead six w/
pistons as big as
Texas flapjacks
Bought in '74 from
first owner who
used it to transport
flagstone from
Flagstaff AZ
to Redondo Beach CA

Even in the
warmth of afternoon
the air has that chill

of mountain crispness
making one appreciate
the sun's warmth
unlike Los Angeles
where you feel as if
you are being cooked
very
slowly

EL AY to Flag in 7 hours
no excessive speeds nearly
500 miles of desert and scrub
Slight vibration in front end
at 65 mph – nothing new
decent gas mileage – why worry?
My hosts are two poets:
Uncle Don and Chaparral
(refugees from Los Angeles
five months in this hideaway)
nestled into the woods
within walking distance
of old downtown
tourist mecca and curio hidy-ho!

Uncle Don looking very much like old-timey western
character actor and safari guide has agreed to put
this raggedy traveler up for a night or two at his
rustic cabin in the pines – under certain conditions:
no boozing
no smoking
no combustibles
no red meat.
Flexible omnivore me
philosophy of denial
alls I ask for is a place to lay my head
and I'm home.
We sit up after dinner and trade
on the commodity that joins us:
THE POEM.
And discuss recent issues of Lummox Journal
(the other commodity that links us).
Lummox Journal Subscription Proviso:
"Subscribers are hereby advised that in
the event of an adventure (as in road

On/Off the Beaten Path

*excursion field trip or walkabout) by the
Lummox Raindog they can expect to be
asked to provide sleeping space (driveway
yard sofa or spare bed) for a night or two.
Most subscribers will be safe from these
mental molestations by dint of distance
of location but all subscribers should be
aware of this clause"*
Lummox subscribers are the
stepping stones by which I ford
the stream of consciousness.
Strangers when we meet —
Friends when we part.
The Lummox affords an odd
sense of anonymous intimacy.
Its monthly rumblings from Raindog
painting a picture of...what?
A man on the go?
Or a man going down slow?
Not the portrait of a man insane
enough to live with beasts?
Must be fairly safe as folks
keep letting this man enter
their lives and accept the
pleasure of their hospitality.

Activist / Environmentalists
D & C stand resolute like Earth
Day celebrants back in "We can
do it!" nineteen fucking seventy
Fighting the good fight against
corporate greed and cronyism
"Boycott Barnes & Noble"
"Ban Nuclear Dumping"
An unbridled passion for the
natural realm that leaves me
feeling guilty and somewhat
ashamed of my cynicism
Earlier
before dinner
D&C go forth to do battle
with the Flagstaff City Council.
I follow – out of curiosity.
Standing alone outside City

Hall in late afternoon —
more than air beginning to chill —
that "something" still flirting
with my peripheral vision
I become aware of the light.
"Oh the light is really beautiful
out there, you'll see"
I know
I've already been here before
seen the light above Abiquiu
where Georgia O'Keeffe
saw it finally die away.
Already seen it reflected
across the mesas just south of Four Corners.
Already wondered how something
that's invisible can be beautiful
And
Yet
As I look upon leaf / life-less
Birch trees
Their branch tips
seemingly wrapped in
gold foil I find myself
agreeing the light
is
beautiful.
The trees seem to radiate light
"...luminous beings all."
Whatever the reason
the light is
truly
beautiful
up here
A kind of natural studio
of radiant light
And now I remember that
it is this natural repository
of wonder that keeps drawing me
back to these southwestern desert
states of mind
year after year.
It is the same light that drew
D.H. Lawrence to Ghost Ranch
and Juan Carlos to Santa Fe:

On/Off the Beaten Path

a shimmering essence that begs to be captured
and yet cannot be caught
even on film.
Yet one must settle at a hint
or suggestion of the effect of this land
on one's brainpan...
even the notion of progress
in the political arena
is as illusory as a mirage.
The only solid form one can count on
is the bond that is forged in friendship
good will and respect.

Riding through town in the
doorway of an empty boxcar
Sleep calls to me insistently
like the blast of a train horn
until I can no longer ignore it
and must succumb.
Don says the different trains have
different "calls" like birds but I
am unused to them and night
becomes a long *Woooo-ooo-oooo*
and *clanka-clank-clank*
punctuated by brief moments of
silence.
And yet
I sleep
and wake to
dawn's rosy glow
and early morning chill.

It is an oddly cold place
surrounded on three sides by desert
and an old volcano on the fourth
its ancient fingers of lava resting easy
on a sandy bed at ease at 7000 feet.

And now the day begins in earnest
and a chorus of tweet-tweets, chirp-chirps
and caw-caws supersedes the
metallic industry of the trains.
I lay in bed absorbing the transition
and reading the work of Roger Taus

(Echo Park, CA) and John Macker
(Las Vegas, NM) – poets I've met
or hope to meet – former & latter.
Ahead of me:
300 miles of whining highway
ABQ via towns further ignored
by progress –
Pinta
Navajo
Sanders
(Where the Whiting Bros once
ruled both the gas and lodging game)
Lupton
Manuelito
Gallup
(A town that looks worse than Tijuana
as if civilization had stopped at the
intersection of Highway 666 – the Navajo
Highway that slides down the border
of AZ/NM from Shiprock and old Route 66
to puke up a bad truck-stop burrito)
Thoreau
(A town of contemplatives?)
Blue Water
(A trading post in ruins and two giant arrows
sticking out of the ground like forgotten
lawn darts – "Genuine Indian Artifacts"
complete with absurdly decorated concrete
teepees – not a hogan in sight)
Milan
(red cliffs – a prison – the biggest
truck stop I've been to since Cabazon –
strong coffee – sardines & crackers –
trucks wheezing by)
Mesita
(the white church on the hillside – a
vaguely familiar landmark at last)
Albuquerque
(ABQ).

Mesas cling to the distant horizon
as I head east towards NM border.
Mesas of Hopi and Navajo Reservations...
Where coyote trickster first dogged my

On/Off the Beaten Path

       trail back in '74
       where adventures began and ended
       along with meetings of remarkable
       men and women: Thomas Banyacya,
       Mina Lanza, Sylvia Richards, John
       Nomura, Sari Staggs
       all but last two gone from this earth
       and in some ways
       all gone to me now.

       And still
       something darts
       through the scrub.
       Some kind of shadow...

       Long hours on lonely roads:
       the mind wanders around looking
       for something to do.
       Inevitably, it comes back to the familiar
       stripping away the layers of things
       onion-like – peeling
       back the skins.
       I think of Don and Chaparral
       and Luis Campos and Todd
       Moore and Roger Taus and
       John Macker and Mark Weber
       and all the other poets I know
       (and don't know)
       All of them working
       quietly laboring away in service of
       THE POEM – before work or
       after, doing what must be done
       so they can continue to make
       the holy POEM even if said
       holy POEM is just a few sad
       lines long.
       I'm thinking how the poet
       cannot hope to make a living
       (unlike other artists) solely from
       this craft without dependence
       on grants or fellowships or prizes

or teaching or betting on the
horses or trust funds or con games.
Few just write (or exist to just
write) THE POEM.
It's crazy.
I'm crazy.

And yet...

In the god-forsaken badlands
that separate Lupton (to the west)
and Gallup (to the east)
one does not expect to find anything
of note, much less remarkable.
Perhaps it's the way the desert
camouflages its constant state of movement —
hidden from our casual glimpses out
across the seemingly endless *nothing* –
that sets us up for the next surprise...
A land devoid of definition
a blur of shapes
of dirty / washed-out colors.

                                        And yet

a sudden splatter of
confetti-white
shatters a cool sky –
a cluster of motion
that blinks on...
then off. Then on...
Then off!
It is only a flock
of white birds flying
in a wide circle but
in this endless caged
monotony of road noise
and white line fever
It is an aerial ballet
exquisite.

White freckles against
a blue sky.

On/Off the Beaten Path

Pot holes and the blast of
a semi bring me back to
the business at hand.

A cobalt blue snow-capped peak
rises out of the horizon line
like an old tit or a
compressed vision of Mt. Fuji.
In the distance
a smear of white hovers close to the
tanned earth as if someone has
erased part of the sky and left
the white paper visible behind it.
The air is hot in spite of the
altitude – there are hardly any
shimmers on the asphalt.
Hardly any notice of the way
the land falls away to the south
the desert sloping down from the
Continental Divide (tailbone
of the Rockies at this point).

Nothing but ABQ ahead.

You can hear it before you get there.
KUNM plays an eclectic mix of sound
from Country to Classical to Jazz to Rock & Roll.
I caught some show with a lot of
weird Country tunes on it and some
gal asking if the listeners wanted to hear
the Bumblebee Tuna Song or
something like that.
Coming to your radio soon –
another pledge-drive.
So I hear ABQ about 40 miles before I see it.
Then you start up this long grade
and you go up..up...up and just as you crest
the top you see
           oh my god!
                 ABQ is
                      HUGE!

Last time I was here
(on my way to El Rito – to the

north above Española)
some 17 years ago
I know I woulda noticed it
even if my vision was somewhat
impaired from being a tad lubricated.
Be that as it may
ABQ sprawls across the valley
I-40 dividing it like a piece of
straw stuck to a concrete road-apple.
ABQ – 600,000 strong and 6,000 feet above sea level
(six is the number of the day hereabouts).

ABQ – forget the mountains just
on the eastern edge of town and
you could think you were in
some part of the San Gabriel Valley
not in some western shoot-em-up
burg out in Nooooh Mexico.
I had a different look in mind
(seventeen years notwithstanding).
More like Santa Fe or Taos.

Nearly four years ago Todd Moore
and I began corresponding back
and forth on a regular basis.
He contributes to the journal
every now and then and
his presence is always appreciated
by the readership and staff.
Published two of his books.
Felt I knew him pretty well
but wanted to "press the flesh"
and hang out with the guy
(Again the Lummox Clause).

I pictured Todd and wife Barbara
living in a nice little pueblo-style
two bedroom adobe job on San
Pedro Street
(sounds pretty rustic right?)
Not so.
Strictly suburban daddy-o.
Unassuming and anonymous
I drove by it twice.

On/Off the Beaten Path

No one would ever suspect
that the guy who wrote
The Corpse is Dreaming
lived there and ate there
and worked out the crazy
catechism that is "Sundance":
a mixture of knives
literature and leather-tough
characters from his past.
Sundance writes THE POEM –
it's raw and ragged and sometimes
it won't stop bleeding...
It bleeds because at its core
all his poems have a heart
(a heart that must pump because
that's what hearts do — pump – otherwise
a heart is just a pound of meat).
So – of course – I expect Sundance
to have that air of machismo
that one sees swaggering around the El Lay
Western hangouts.
No dice pilgrim.
Sundance is a quiet guy who
speaks intensely about THE POEM
who bristles when he thinks about
those who pretend and practice at
the craft...

So I – the stranger – enter the life of this man.
It's Tuesday afternoon and he greets me
and we might as well be two old friends
getting together for a weekly card game
as easy as it is – this first actual meeting.
Six hours later
in the guest bed
making notes
I wonder what
I was worried about?
No te preocupes, eh?
(No worries)
Except for the accursed shadow
that dogs my every move.
Someday I'm gonna be found out.
Someday the phony-baloney from L.A

will be unmasked...
I suspect that the face under the
mask is the same face *of* the mask
therefore – no mask at all
but the old training does not die
easy – the old training does not go gentle
into that good night...
No it rages
        RAGES
AGAINST
THE LIGHT.
Change does not come easy.
It's far easier to change
your oil
or your sox
or your mate.

Still
one must push on
right?

So, Todd and I hit it off
in grand style and I'm glad
I made the trek – thinking
"if nothing else works out
the trip will still be worth it..."

the harbinger

I plan to hang out with Todd
tomorrow & try to hook up with
Mark Weber – local luminary
(KUNM jazz DJ and better known
poet than Todd – Mark would not
welcome this comparison as we are all
in this together – the fact remains that
Mark is more visible whatever the reason).
Beyond that I have no plans.
So it's some light reading and it's lights out.

Until 2 a.m.
when a strange dream
awakens me and I
cannot fall back to sleep.

On/Off the Beaten Path

Is it insomnia or time
management redefined?
Sometimes the drummer
calls you out at the odd hour.

So I'm reading Macker's
Burroughs in Santo Domingo
and the imagery is bouncing
inside me like an ancient ache –
not even sure if I get the meaning of
what I'm reading –
but imagery is funny that way
and suddenly...
suddenly I sense a rhythm
developing in me like a sine
wave – aftershock – hurtling
through the bedrock of memory.
I pause
shifting in this
borrowed bed
to slip from
this knowledge
(know *ledge*?)
and flutter my
eyelids back to sleep –
per chance *not* to dream
for it was dream that started
me down this avenue
in the first place.

I hear Todd in the next room
sleep not easy for him either
"up every two hours out of
habit – years of ulcers" dictating
sleep-pattern. I struggled for
years with insomnia back 17
years ago – 3 a.m. every night –
pickled liver kicking into action.
Still happens on occasion
the mind being a simple thing
easily riled or excited.
The mind as a young child –
easily moved to boisterous behavior.

In the dream I am telling a friend
about a haunted tree.
The tree has it out for me – is fixated
on me as being the source of its troubles.
My friend is skeptical.
I say "I'll show you" and throw a book
at the base of the tree.
A woman picks it up and takes it inside
a house that suddenly appears behind the tree.
"Now watch."
Suddenly a black book
(the size of a video tape)
comes flying out of the tree
like an enraged blackbird just
missing my head.
My friend jumps back and
looks at me as if she's seeing
me for the first time.
A voice in the tree says "Brujo".
It is Todd's voice.
I wake to my pounding heart.

In the morning over coffee & toast
I relate the dream to Todd.
He is pleased.
His being pleased makes me
uneasy.
I know –
no
I sense –
that the shadow is
closing on me and
now I realize that Todd
senses this too.
I look at him in a different light
as though he is now teacher & I
student – studying on this problem
the problem of the shadow and what
the shadow will bring to me
to be examined and
understood.
And innocently I enter into this
unaware that my senses are being honed –
tooled-up and re-calibrated for the task ahead.

On/Off the Beaten Path

    We set off to 'tour' ABQ

    a memory of something 80 proof rolls across my tongue

    Todd takes me to Central Avenue
    (every town must have one I think).
    It is to Route 66 what L.A.'s Sepulveda
    Blvd. is to Highway One.
    Many an Okie passed this way before
    either of us were born
    and I guess I must have passed
    this way near the mid-century mark
    (but as Hoosier – not Okie) at the
    tail-end of the WW2 migration west.

    Central cleaves ABQ and ABQ culture
    clean in half – separating the wheat
    from the chaff – at the knees.

    "This has always been a rough
    and tumble town. Used to be part of
    the old 'Outlaw Trail' – coming up
    outta Mexico on its way to Colorado/
    Utah. The Wild Bunch used it as
    a hideout for a time and old Sheriff Earp
    spent some of his pension here.
    It's seen more'n its share of
    gunfights n' hangin's. And that
    was the old days!"
    Nowadays
    the men favor
    a cold-hearted
    passion and exercise
    it freely and "with prejudice."
    Passion is an equal
    opportunity master
    favoring no race
    no creed
    no religion
    or sexual preference.
    So the Asians
    the Blacks
    the Indians
    the Latinos

On/Off the Beaten Path

the Whites
can act up at will.
It's a hell of a town...

Central descends towards the
Rio Grande and so do the lifestyles.
Near the top of the hill –
a nice blend of White suburbia.
Halfway down the social strata
begins a downward slide.
Indians "just off the Rez" mingle
with street people (of unidentifiable
national origin except as citizens of Dirt).
Hot Rodders race through traffic
their identity linked so completely to their
"rides" that "hangin' offense" may become
the fashionable justice option once again.
Blacks and Asians labor quietly in
neighborhoods off Central –
working towards a memory of a life
bettered while their kids join gangs
and raise hell.

"You don't want to come here at night."
And I wonder if you have to teleport
into the hip spots since they're
surrounded by the bad-ass gangs.

Did you see that? What was it?

Todd and I go to meet Mark.
I realize I was imagining Todd in Mark's house –
a nice little (sweet some would say) white-
washed adobe L shaped house with
an inviting garden and built-in BBQ

And I remember a house in Chimayo
across a small wooden bridge – under the
shade of a Cottonwood –
its leaves rustling in the afternoon wind.

Mark – the reason I heard of Todd
in the first place (again the Lummox
connection) – looks a lot like a beefy

On/Off the Beaten Path

... A HOUSE IN CHIMAYPO ACROSS
A WOODEN BRIDGE ... A
COTTONWOOD TREE FOR SHADE,
IT'S LEAVES RUSTLING IN THE WIND

version (too many pancakes?) of the
character actor Jack Elam and
a bit like a raven
the way he cocks his
head back and looks at you like he
could be measuring your worth
vis-a-vis some other bauble he's
been thinkin' about obtaining.
Mark is the storyteller – each story
a piece in the puzzle that will
eventually portray "Big Web."
Seems like each story starts with
"That was the time I was loaded
out of my mind..."
A time of wild darkness.

On/Off the Beaten Path

And my own time of darkness returns
my adventures overlaying Mark's
becoming the same tale told from
two different vantage points.

The stories continue over lunch
at some soup & salad joint in a
strip mall not far from Mark's
Noooh Mexican hideaway.
Like two war veterans
Mark & Todd trade stories.
But the stories become a drone
that lulls me off to another time
pulling me back to another trip

the shadow
again

and I resist it
but just barely.

I know I am hitting my limit of ABQ
that my interest in being here is fading
(in part because of the other memories
that are beginning to surface – I'm thinking
I can out-run them if I get a good head
start in the morning – kind of slip out
while nobody's looking... hit the road
running).
"I've done what I came to do."
My excuse.

More stories and poetry on Todd's patio
the patient unblinking eye of the Cyclops
named Sony recording their words.
Reminiscence about fallen friends
of Kell and Judson and others coming
and going before my time in this life
this life of poets and I am suddenly moved
by the simple grace of these two men
and the miracle of their lives.
And just as quickly
I am ashamed of my own

On/Off the Beaten Path

    hesitation.
    I have lived many lives –
    long enough to have many regrets.
    I may have decided too late to
    hold back
    no more...

    a fragment of a dream comes to me:
    I'm racing across the desert
    on the eastern side of Joshua Tree
    hurtling towards a place called Pinto Basin.
    It is a place of dark doings and I am going
    against my will...

    Bernalillo
    (must)
    La Cienega
    Santa Fe
    (keep)
    Tesque
    Pojonque
    Santa Cruz
    (going)
    Española
    (ignore it)
    Hernandez
    (Turn off for El Rito – I blow past it
    on my way to some *other* Pinto Basin)
    Abiquiu
    (Should have stopped here to bless
    the front end of my car – to bless my own
    twisted heart – at least to see the last home
    of the painter Georgia O'Keeffe)
    Cebolla
    Tierra Amarilla
    (home of the county seat – where militant
    Latinos shot up the court house back in the 70s
    in a Noooh Mexican-style protest – real
    Pancho-fuckin' Via baby "Viva la Raza!")
    Los Brazos
    Chama
    (8000 feet – snow on the ground – gateway
    to the happy hunting grounds – *17* miles to
    the Colorado border)

On/Off the Beaten Path

Lumberton
(ten houses – a post office – an abandoned
market – a pack of dogs crossing the road
with time on their side)
Dulce
(across the top of Noooh Mexico – frozen Rockies
floating in a blue sea of Colorado air just to the north)
Blanco
(Apache Rez – dogs or coyotes loping along
the highway: two lanes of cracked asphalt
deserted except for road kill and sudden pickup
on my tail – hardhatted passengers looking ragged
and menacing – front end vibration getting stronger)
Bloomfield
Farmington

... SOME GIGANTIC SCULPTURE –
AS IF RODIN HAD MODELED
HIS BRONZE OF BALZAC AFTER IT

On/Off the Beaten Path

Kirtland
Fruitland
Shiprock
(the guts of a long since eroded volcano
stands on the horizon like some gigantic
sculpture – as if Rodin had modeled his
bronze of Balzac after this black mass of lava)

Teec Nos Pos AZ
(exit to Four Corners Landmark)
Red Mesa
I have a vague sense that Pinto Basin
the metaphor that it stands for
is close by: the cracked asphalt
this desolate and broken ribbon
crossing the scrub-lands like a
long shadow
I hurtle across it
alone
moving ahead
the car vibrating
like in the dream
rattling into the falling sun
into the silent roaring
space
the ugliness that waits
between worlds
between words

Mexican Water
(backside of the mesas – all Navajo Rez)
Tes Nez Iah
(exit south to Canyon de Chelly – *Cottonwoods*
breathing heavy in late afternoon thunder storm –
Spider Rock standing defiantly at canyon fork)
Dinnehotso
(the Three Sisters watch over the valley
waiting for someone to return and relieve
them – "ok girls, shift's over.")
Kayenta
(exit to Monument Valley – car running really
rough now – feels like the front wheels are
going to fall off unless I keep going on – plunging
into the dusk – too bad I really wanted to see

*I REMEMBER THE STARS
DISAPPEARING oVER THE EDGE
oF THE MESA . . .*

the monuments again)
Tsogi
Cow Springs
(somewhere in the fading dusk a strange apparatus
hangs off the mesa – Black Mesa – where Peabody
Coal strip-mines on a gazillion tons of the sooty
fossil fuel – the stuff dropping off the mesa on a
conveyor belt that looks like Satan's own roller
coaster and is sent up over the highway and into
a trio of silos as big as any Air Force wet-dream erection
for shipment to markets at all points of the compass)
Red Lake
(exit to Hopi Rez – I would search for
the happy camping grounds of bygone years
but it is too dark this road too narrow and the
car is driving so rough that I feel I'm making it

On/Off the Beaten Path

go by sheer force of will – by the knot in my
stomach and the whites of my knuckles)

I remember the stars disappearing <u>over</u> the
edge of the mesa on a certain night in 1975
with snow on the ground as far as you could
see in the inky blackness and a kind Hopi Indian
woman named Mina Lanza giving me hot
chocolate to thaw out my bones after driving
7 Hopi elders back to Second Mesa from L.A.

I make a silent prayer for Sylvia
Thomas Banyacya & Mina
all gone now
lost in those stars
over the edge
out of reach.

Tuba City
Stop at first motel (Dineh) – Navajo Rez
500 + mile loop up one side of NM across the top
and down into AZ – the car feels like
a B-25 returning to base after a bad
mission over Bremen – shot to hell –
rattling and shaking violently – maybe the
landing gear is down maybe not –
the pilot is just about dead – the bed looks
mighty nice but the road takes hours to die away
and dawn comes fast and furiously)
Cameron
(entire desert appears to be sculpted
in red meringue in morning light –
not)
Gray Mountain
(sure)
Antelope Hills
(I'll)
Flagstaff
(make it – to Uncle Don's and then to mechanic –
where the news is not good: CV Joints must
be replaced – cost: the rest of the budget for
the trip – "hey man you got the million
dollar wound! You're going home!")
Lucky me.

On/Off the Beaten Path

Yet somewhere back out there
the shadow pants beside
the road
It will slide sideways
back into the bush
and melt into the land
I know I will return
(look what it did for MacArthur)
I'll have to and I will
have to stalk the shadow.
                        Something grinning at me
like a silhouette reflected
in the glazed eye of a dead
mule deer (glimpsed in a ditch
beside the road near Lumberton)
floating in the pupil's dark pool
a figure – dark and menacing
a burly som-bitch
Waiting
for my return.

So am I.

ROAD KILL

The Author at an early age, worshipping at the altar of the Great Chrome God, BUICK ROADMASTER

Photo: Tom Armstrong

Introduction

All journeys begin with nervous anticipation: what's around the next bend? What will happen out there? Will I be able to rise to the challenges I encounter? Life is a crapshoot after all. Sometimes you win, sometimes you don't. The trick is to take whatever comes and make the best of it. Travel is movement and movement is fluid, so be open to change, your plans are not written in stone, are they?

This journey encompassed a 3247mile jaunt across the western U.S. from Long Beach, CA to Port Angeles, WA via Route 1, Hwy 101 and Interstate 5 (with a few side-trips). Sixteen days – undertaken between September 5th and the 21st. It would have been a daunting trip under normal circumstances, but, even more so, because of events that followed the morning of the 11th.

Many thanks must go out to my friends along the way who happily provided a warm meal, a place to sleep and good conversation; especially Greg and Colleen of Port Angeles who put up with my eccentricities during my four day visit (the longest stop on this whirl-wind tour as it turned out).

ROAD KILL

The desire to get off to a good start
Is the root of all superstition
Yet here I am having second thoughts
Every other second about this trip
One that I made fourteen years ago
In a '54 Chevy ¾ ton flatbed
Without a care in the world
And nary a worry in my head
Or the one I made in '77 in
That '63 Rambler American
The one with the bad
Throw-out bearing and the
Bob Jones University sticker
On the rear window
Of course I was younger
Then and less tied
Down to whatever I'm
Tied to now
Still
For weeks leading up to this
"Jaunt" that little voice
in my head keeps muttering about
an impending danger…
OUT THERE
Like a hushed whisper in church
OUT THERE
Be on your toes
Baby be on your toes
Like Westside story
Something's coming yes it is
So I packed my car with
All the accoutrements
Of a traveling poetry road show:
Books catalogs flyers
Clothes sleeping bag
Food water music cameras
Maps tools new tires
Loaded for bear or whatever
And headed to the 'jump-off'
A reading on Tuesday night in
Beautiful cracktown

Roadkill

        Tujunga CA at the public library
        Clear across town from
        My beautiful cracktown
        Of Long Beach and under a
        Pale moon rising pink and
        Full into a sweltering Indian
        Summer night found myself
        At a reading that no one
        Save one brave soul
        (Thank you Chris)
        Bothered to attend
        "I don't understand it
        We always have a good turnout
        For these readings"
        I have heard this too
        Many times to even worry
        About it should I tell
        Her that I never draw a crowd
        Couldn't draw a crowd even
        If I jumped off a building
        Into noonday pedestrian lunch hour
        After waiting for forty minutes
        We declare the corpse cold
        And head off into the night
        The host and audience go home
        And I north
        To my first destination
        Of Ojai to sleep at Peter Sims'
        House (the backwoods of Ojai
        Hillbilly country style – Miner's Oaks)
        Traveling the road from Tujunga
        Crossing the Eye Five to
        Catch the 126 W through
        Cracktowns Santa Paula Ventura
        Dark road lit by
        Pink moon
        Pink Floyd
        Wish You Were Here
        Cue the soundtrack
        For this rolling Theater of
        One playing for the next
        Few weeks out here on
        Desolation road
        Coming past a theater of you

Roadkill

Watch for it don't miss it
Tonight's feature:
Chasing the insight
At Pete's place another Pete
Waits for me from Massachusetts
Another poet another day right
Peter Frawley poet pauper inner
Space traveler art soldier of fortune
Impaled on the glorious
Pike of love resting up out here
In California recovering and licking
His wounds before heading
Home to the east coast
And we talk
And talk
And talk of the poem
The Smithing of it
The hammering out and repeated
Forging of it in the fire
The dipping into water
Hard work this crafting of words
Into something that's intelligible even
If only to the wordsmith
All the while the pink moon
Sails overhead and
Is well on its downward glide
When my head finally lands
On my pillow the cacophony of
Nature singing me to sleep and
Quick as a wink I'm having cereal
Orange juice tea and making notes
In the road journal
From which this narrative is loosely
Based Peter still wrapped in the
Arms of Morpheus
So with a note on the table
I gas up with the sun on my left shoulder
Head towards and past
Santa Barbara Goleta Buelton
Home of Anderson's Split Pea Soup
How many trips up North riding my
Thumb have I stopped here to
Gorge on All You Can Eat green

Roadkill

Soup and sourdough bread
Still on the One-Oh-One speeding past
Santa Maria San Luis Obispo
The road still familiar still known
Not the perilous road of distant memory
Or even but not on this trip
Unknown origins
Perilous because the whine of tire
On asphalt becomes a chorus
Humming in your ear white noise that
Can lull the unsuspecting traveler
Onto the soft-shoulder demise of carelessness
Even the unknown can be known
As you become one with your ride
Moving in concert with it becoming an
Extension of your will desires curiosity
The trusted mount that serves as long as
You keep an eye on the fuel oil and coolant
You and The Ride becoming a
Rhythm working its way across
The back of the asphalt snake
Wending your way northward
Almost out of the northern suburbs
Of Los Angeles debating about the Big
Sur route of HWY One or staying inland
Past King City and Camp Hunter Ligget
Looking rundown under Bush 41's
Peace Dividend neglected and
Dilapidated its barracks silent the
Motor pool empty save for grease spots
Dirty testimony to the once thriving
Post past the long stretch of oil fields
Where 101 once was a two-lane on
East side of the valley and a much younger
Raindog traveled past old barns with
Tobacco ads painted on sideboards
With the ghost of Karen Lang riding
Shotgun this leg of journey I speed along
Behind a Semi with black mud flaps
Tossing to-and-fro like window shades
Flapping in the breeze later another Semi with
Exhaust pipes a good eight feet above the
Cab reminding me of a giant red bull with
Burnished chrome longhorns (I catch up with

Roadkill

This truck again near the Oregon border) I
Head towards Salinas and the three
Sans: Jose Francisco and (next stop)
Rafael where I'm to meet
Brother Chris for next overnighter
Traveling through the West Bay like
My last run up here in '99 I again
Notice the 'gentrification' (as urban
Planners would say) of almost every square
Inch from San Jose northward as
Commerce makes its run at 'sprawl'
Status gobbling up the Whisky Gulch's
Dogpatch's and other urban eccentricities
A hunger for consistency and uniformity
That is never satisfied never tiring of the
Unrelenting sameness as I run through
Palo Alto I dimly recall a sleepy college town
(Stanford) with streets lined with trees
and an easy leather elbowed comfort
the 101 flowing gently through town
Four lanes of motoring pleasure now
Eight lanes of rush cascading like a
Mad river of steel and rubber
Through a corridor of cement cast
In the image of stone as if the cars
And drivers are to be herded out of
Town as quickly as possible dumped
Onto the flats near Sea Tac south of SanFran
Daly City the old Candlestick Park *now   named
After some public utility* The Cow Palace up
Into The City dumped kerrplop onto the
Streets of San Francisco (what's Mike
Stone up to these days) to wend and fight
The old 101 route through town to
That glorious orangish-red steel spanning
The gateway to The Bay here the wind
Blows endlessly gusting strong enough to
Create unscheduled lane changes or
Parting hats from the unwary to sleep
With the fishes or convicts who live by
The water on scenic drive North Bay side
Just a hop-skip-and-a jumper or two from
My next destination
Again urban sprawl but now cleverly disguised as

Roadkill

Woodsy homeland spreads here even though
Treeline and marshes hamper development
San Rafael looks as congested as my last visit
I make a bee line for Crescent where the bro
Will meet me but as usual I'm early by at
Least an hour so it's back down to java hut
For herb tea and more jottings in The Book
Local headcase with a deer in the
Headlights look *too many years of*
Acid he tells me strikes up with me mostly
Carrying the conversation he waits for
A ride to pick him up and transport him
Down the peninsula to the afore-
Mentioned stadium to bear witness
To the Giants in action he is a man
Possessed by baseball and the National
Geographic and of course the other
National pastime gawking at women
We pause to appreciate one across the room
Taking a big stretch her blouse pulling
Tight across her chest we exchange
Nods his one of innocence mine not
So pure of intention *he's got it pretty*
Good I'm thinking later I'm back at my
Brother's house amid the chaos of
His two dogs and the US Open where
Two 'old' men battle on clay in NY NY
It's good to see him again even if all we
Do is watch ESPN for three or four hours
It's what we brothers do each visit
Our Zazen a sitting meditation our koan
Having to do with the line fault next morning
Early sleeping only five hours (a pattern
Developing) I smell my brother's first cigarette
His 'mooring' smoke tying him to the waking
World which means out the door to work
By 5: 30 AM to his 60 hour a week job as
Carpenter in SF and the means by
Which he can afford *the overpriced*
Shack he calls home his safe haven
From the obstacles to his hard rules:
Work play drink and live hard he's convincing
But I've seen and known many who
Would whip his butt still he's a grown man

Roadkill

(Though younger than I) and has chosen
This path of (lesser) resistance I decide
It's not my place to speakup even though
I know this path like the back of
My hand *on my return trip I wish I had
Spoken up* by now the dogs are up and off
On early AM walkies the shack fills with
The smell of coffee one burnt smell
Eclipsing another amidst great hubbub
And a hearty *see you later* he's gone
The roar of his engine fading into a
Pair of dogs barking their farewells
And God speed and soon it will be my turn
Too easing into traffic on 101 cruising
Past the southbound 'parking lot'
Grateful to be going in the wrong
Direction (true to form as always) next
Stop McKinleyville *no statue of the
Man in town* where my dad lives with
His Bonnie her brother Kenny *recovering
From a tough patch* a big-ass Great Dane
Named after a moon of Jupiter Calisto Blue
Once you leave behind the little towns
That aren't anymore and head up into
Timberlands past Willets you begin to
Experience the cutting-edge of highway
Driving ALA the modern super road a
Conglomerate of cantilevers and four
Lane luxury where trees are glimpsed
At a safe distance unlike the stretches that
Follow where old 101 two lane winds through
Redwood groves crowding the shoulder
Close enough to steal a mirror if given
Half a chance where trees become a blur
Green punctuated with brown and the
Occasional curio stand featuring any &
Everything carved from redwood burls
Unique Indian trinkets and good god
Almighty the wonder of Indian Casinos
One million dollar Black Jack tables one
Proclaims snippets of memories of last
Run up this highway to visit dad what
Six or seven years ago produces dim
Familiarity with this long and lonely

Roadkill

Stretch of lushness lost under the
Big blue (not IBM) sky canopy only one
Memory comes back at a gas stop outside
Rio Dell company town houses barracks
Huge lumber mill town stopped here for
Gas coming back south year unknown
It was wet and gray there could have been fog
I don't recall everything was dark and
In memory darker still there was a face
A smear of light on a dark canvas today
Finds Rio Dell under sunlight I am running
Down the mountains and out onto the
Wild flats along the Pacific Ocean Fortuna
Lays to the west Eureka to the north dad's
Just north of Altuna *statue of the Prez is*
Here for some reason living in a roomy tract
Home of his own making I mean he really
Built the sucker built the whole tract in fact
My pops the developer my bro the carpenter
Me the eccentric no wonder we don't
Sit down and have those heart-to-hearts
Like mi hermano what does he think of me
Not any worse than I do hopefully I only ask for
A fair shot a small parity we watch the US Open
Eat dinner and settle down to discuss life
As only we know it I'm just happy to be here
With him even for only these hours we are
Eye-to-eye and worth the fifty years it took
To get here I'm mostly surprised at my non-
Chalance about this *well it took what it took*
This is more important to me than the
Who dids and the to whom or why game
My dad older than his own dad now by many
Years isn't much different otherwise he's
Still dreaming big and living bigger than might
Be wise but he's used to having it his way or
The highway which calls to me I see my dad
Will maybe outlive me I must move on the long
Road to Eugene/Springfield Oregon is already
Buzzing with anticipation a two-lane road
Previously unknown to me 199 East to eye-
Five then eye-five north to visit Leno
Missed him in Eureka lives with Marjorie
His mom a pistol and sharp too *I'm in my*

Roadkill

Eighties you know she confides the pair of them
Make for an interesting memory before I can get
There I must stop and go my way across California
Oregon border and stop and go my way through
Southern ORYGON behind road crews
Two guys with clipboards supervising one guy
With a shovel and one guy with a stop/slow
Sign they call it Highway Rehabilitation
Do the roads go to group therapy too

I call it a pain in the ass still
The gorges are gorgeous the rivers are idyllic
And the cracktowns appear sleepy and safe
Even Rogue River a town that didn't exist
As far as I can remember back when Karen
Lang and I trekked west along the great Rogue
River Trail a grand adventure done on a whim
My gut fear completely ignored for a week
On our own in the wilderness ahhh youth
Ahh too bad youth grows up and doubt
Takes over one bright spot though the
Novelty of full service gas stations where
You cannot *under penalty of law* pump
Your own gas strange times gas costs more
Up here than back home up here in
This tree-hugger paradise where even tree
Stumps are plucked from dirty hillsides by
Man's problem-solving brain all that smarts
And we still can't figure out how to work

Roadkill

Out our differences except with a club
Leno works nights he's also an insomniac
So it works out for him I'm early to his house
I sit in my car outside his house in
Springfield or *Springahoma* as he calls it
Could be a cracktown save for the fact it
Butts up (uncomfortably so) tight against Eugene
Real Andy of Mayberry *if you know what I mean*
Not Leno he of Pygmy Forest Press a force to
Be reckoned with a chain-smoker and spouter
Of hyped up manic ideas strong opinions
Knowledgeable like my friend Todd Moore
A guy you could trust with your back a
Stand up human being makes me wish I had
Gotten into the publishing game sooner (
Because that's how I've met all these guys
Not as just as a poet) so I coulda met Leno
Sooner than later must get to bed early so I
Can get up early Leno won't get up to see me
Off because he *never does anything special for*
Members of the family guess I've been adopted
Hit the couch at eleven only to wake up at two
Thirty too damn early but I can't sleep with all
These ideas and free associations bouncing
Around in my head plus a bowl of ice cream
With Leno doesn't help but the camaraderie
Is worth the lost sleep it's seems so easy I look
Around the room with it's checkered tablecloth
And china curio cabinet and all the simple
Pleasures that one can gather up over the years
And I marvel that from these simple surroundings
Comes such a force of creativity and poetics
Still I can't sleep even amid such wonder
A man still has to get up and head north
In the impending squint of first-light but
Sleep is in short supply so I give up on finding
It tonight get up and get ready Leno is up
And we part company more friends than
Before the five-thirty streets dead first
Inkling *we're [not] in Kansas [anymore]*
These are streets of another time quiet
Streets quiet like the early morning chill
Like the dim countryside whipping past
At seventy five mile per hour

Roadkill

Scrapbook
(for LJC)
A house divided / partially mended
Broken chair
Charred door
Window box
Long shadow
Cast unevenly
Through a doorway
Glass table
With water spots
Transient damage
Coffee stains
Unopened pack of smokes
Pot of coffee
Waiting in the dark
Screams in the hallway
Demons at every turn
A cat stretching
Long and slow
Fog in the meadow
Bit of skull
Mementos
Of past lives
What is this crazy need for conversation for
Confirmation that I exist as if a footprint
Isn't enough as if I must make my mark or
Prove I've been this way Orygun slips by
Under cover of dawn I scoot ever closer to
Washington and it's 'stately forests and
Peaceful waterways' my friends in Port
Angeles Greg & Colleen out on errands
When I will arrive later today for now
The sky above and the trees below time
Was I'd pass through feeling out of step
With my surroundings now I seem to be
Merely aware of my disconnection not
Bothered more at ease with my fleeting
Intimacies my just-off-target encounters
Funny how you can fall into a rhythm
With the road it's terrain and routine
For example I decide to take old 101 up
To Port Angeles instead of taking the
More modern cut-off route on the eight

Roadkill

Lane up through Bremerton old two
Lane 101 twists and turns along the
Western bank of Puget Sound on a
Typical Washington morning globs of
Fog hang wet and low fishermen are
Merely silhouettes on mirrors no breath
Of wind except for motorhomes that whip by
On their way north this stretch of road has
Returned to virgin unknown status it being
Nearly twenty-five years since I made it's
Howdy-do like other stretches of 101 and 1
Outside Eureka where you drive slow enough to
See the trees as individuals where they will
Live out their days undisturbed by the cult of
The Saw not so farther north in lumber country
Not tree country where trees are left by the roadside
But thinned to non-existence within yards here
The Logger reigns and the cult and mythology
Of Paul Bunyun and his blue ox Babe his technology
His art his canvas a redwood burl his means of
Expression the chainsaw his knick knacks and curios
Paul reigns supreme even the Indians are represented
Here at least the Hollywood tribe as we all know the
Great Sioux nation spread into NorCal and Orygun
Which is why you can buy war bonnets and teepees
Wampum and totem poles in the roadside shops and
Indian gaming casinos from here to the Canadian
Border the redman's revenge it would seem whatever
You call 'em these are just distractions from the
Meditation of winding road something about winding
Versus straight that makes winding stay with you longer
Something more profound in the *zone* achieved while
Winding over hill and dell there is a naturalness to
The routine check the way ahead check behind check
The mirrors check the gauges the odometer the map
The scenery the other drivers the radio put in a
Tape or turn it off and listen to the car the tires
The world beyond the glass is it all going according
To plan doesn't even matter when you're in the
Zone you are driving on a subconscious level
Leaving your mind to sift through memories
Dormant for years now whipped up like so many
Leaves at roadside memories of trips made
Over the past 30 years or so hitch-hiking to Canada

Roadkill

Or Berkeley (I must have hitched up and down
The California coast twenty times at least – funny
How you don't see too many hitchers anymore)
Motoring around the western US two trips to WY
Two trips to Hopi in NE AZ a trip to Baja San
Felipe to be exact I even drove through the
Cumberland Gap one east coast trip with GMC
Twenty something years ago all the images
Of all the trips begin to swirl in my mind's "I"
Until they become a blur and I don't know
What happened where until I pass a spot
On this road I recognize and another piece
Falls into place Port Angeles hasn't been
Penetrated by The Sprawl yet though
There are signs of its minions camping on
The outskirts of town so far the heart of
Town still beats to its own rhythm still plucks
Along at a slow pace not Springahoma slow
But close enough to piss the hell outta Greg
Whenever we go out on an errand Greg and
Colleen have lived up here since the mid
Seventies this is my third trip driving but
I've flown up here as well (funny how it
Was easier to fly when I was poorer and
Tickets were more expensive) I haven't
Flown in nearly twenty years yet I plan to fly
The end of this month as one would expect
Some things around their house have changed
Even if they've only gotten a few years older
Since I saw them last outwardly Greg seems
The same but he's not there's less of that
Tough as nails mystique that I always looked
Up to in the old days hell we're all getting older
Graying like that old hoss we sure ain't what
We used to be I've been thinking about this
Trip so long that I'm in shock most of the first
Two days at actually being here and then on
The third day I go into a different kind of shock
It begins with a night of recreational jazz courtesy
Of Brian husband of Erin daughter of Colleen
And Greg I sit in with his friends and introduce
Them to recreational jazz poetry courtesy of
LRB 9 Eyes Like Mingus it was great I really
Had a ball hope they did too they were skeptical

Roadkill

About poetry and jazz possible huh next morning
I'm still high from night before gushing to G & C
You shoulda been there it was great so what's
New with you guys and that's when the shit
Hits the fan *oh nothing much just a terrorist*
Attack on NYC blowing up the WTC
?
What
?
Are you kidding me are you just yanking my
Chain or what no it's true check the TV and
There it is an endless loop of smoke towers
The arcing jet fire collapse mushroom cloud
In reverse dirty dust cloud exhaling death
Tickertape parade of sorrow that old sinking
Feeling that comes with any bad news and

CRAP[2]

I'm suddenly dreading the witch hunt that this
Will unleash on anyone vaguely asiatic or dark
Skinned wondering how long the first and
Fourth amendments can hold out who will
Become the next terrorist threat will they be
American all these questions swarming inside
My head distracting me from cnn or msnews
Almost all of Greg's 800 channels are running
Up-to-the-minute-news except the tractor channel
Stunned we sit in silence mugs frozen in mid sip
Sucker punched and shut down no flights
No borders no where to go anyway where
Will the next strike come should I go home
I miss my friends am suddenly homesick
What to do should I stay or should I go
Haven't felt this way since JFK I knew something
Was going to happen but didn't know it
Would be this this horror this catastrophe
America is the whet stone for anyone with
An axe to grind you could almost say we're
The only game in town everyone hates us
It seems not that we haven't and I hate using
We because usually the we who do the things
That make others hate us so much are not
The we of you and I but that other we has
Done a lot of things in the name of us in

Roadkill

The US and now the we that is you and I
We are expected to take a bullet or spore
Or be vaporized in the name of the US of
America I can only stare slackjawed as
This unfolds as I put on a brave face as
I go about my business I still have to
Meet with Tim Scannell and get on with
My trip but I feel less than complete and
The minutes slip by unnoticed and I know
I'll never be the same
Ever
For the next twenty four hours
Whenever I close my eyes the image of
Tower number two collapsing is what I see
First followed by other images of the horror
All screaming in my ear like a chorus of
Ghosts haunting my eyes-wide-open world
Take me home to my own sand box where
I can hide in relative if not naïve security
Take me away from this I don't wanna
Study war no more what is it good for
I'm tired of trying to absorb these images
And numbers tired of this catechism of
Death and destruction this sermon on the
Mound of rubble this trinity of terrorism
There's a new perspective in town we are a
Nation recovering from the collective
Jaw drop the six thousand soul Sunday
Punch and nothing can change that
We have to get up that's what the mayor
Of NYC is saying that's what the president
Is saying up up that's what the ministers
Are saying everyone is saying we have to get
Up and get with the program get right with the
New program make sacrifices *only instead of*
The old sacrifices like rationing or going
Without a few creature comforts this new
Program could include a pogrom or two
Not to mention the serious collapse of an
Economy or two and even the suspension
Of the first and fourth amendments but
Few seem to notice these cracks in the
Façade of lady liberty even after that
Beautiful perfect layer of wonderful—

Roadkill

Don't bother me I'm making a killing in
The stock market— purposeful ignorance
Was also vaporized that morning for the next
Week or so each night as I closed my eyes
To sleep each night as I entered the lobby of
The theater of sleep I had to pass through a
Gallery of images and sounds that had gotten
Stuck in my head from watching and listening to
Cnn msnbc npr and from seeing and scanning
Newspapers in PA and Seattle each and every
Night numbly stumbling towards night-night
A fireman grimacing with pain and disbelief
A face in the smoking ruin of tower one
The words oh my god screamed off camera
An imploding mushroom cloud of gray dust
A president struggling to keep his game face
A smug adversary holding a rifle drinking tea
Grim-faced men who lived and died here for him
The NY skyline with its two front teeth knocked
Out (even twenty billion dollars from the federal
Tooth fairy won't be enough to ease these post-
Partum blues) leaving one with an odd feeling
Whenever it reappears in the backdrop of TV reruns
A mayor who rises from the ashes to redefine
His fate in the waning days of his term of office
And a good god that's a tall building suddenly
Sporting an orangy-red chrysanthemum
Dispassionately I wander past these walls of
Shame to get to sleep to sleep per chance to
Dream ah that is indeed the rub and
Remarkably I do sleep with nary a dream
To scare me awake though I don't sleep for
More than five hours most nights anyway
Maybe there isn't time to process or dream
Maybe I'm not even awake but merely sleep
Walking a zombie in a strange land a land of
Ballet lessons and ice cream sandwiches and
Live jazz and oatmeal and salmon stew and
Croquet one day and silent skies and all this
The next day the new day the day the singing
Cash registers held their breath where a market
Went from bullish to bearish in a heartbeat
Where our forward rush came to a screeching
Halt

Roadkill

Somewhere in all this I visited Tim Scannell
Took my friend Greg along to field all literary
Incoming since my limited GPA of 2.50 and dulled
Down to a nub brain would be no match to Tim a
Scholar and man of unshakeable faith –
Maybe not in God but in the president and
In the US of A – we do not share this opinion
Share few opinions politically in fact except
We agree to disagree our common ground is
The realm of poesy and the tumultuous world
Of the small press (seems but a dream now)
We drive up a long country road past horse
Pastures and the occasional house until Tim's
"Cabin" rolls into view then the greeting the
Tour of the house (lots of big open rooms)
Back outside we set a spell in the three acre
Backyard under a canopy of big leafy trees—
'A lot less than when we moved in 12 years
Ago felled most myself except for the really
Big ones – got help for those' Tim as logger—
And blue autumnal sky just another serene
Day except for cnn murmur on neighbor's TV
And occasional grumbling of Greg over
Logging and environmental issues merely
Hinted at by caretaker Tim I'm just glad I
Wasn't tested for all the info taken in over
The next several hours over tea and coffee

Roadkill

Pie and cigarettes Tim and his wife cheerfully
Chain smoking perhaps wearing their game
Faces a bit too jauntily remnants from their
Recent trips to the UK to meet with lost kin
—Pip pip stiff upper lip eh wot laddy—we all
dealing in our own way me retreating inside
Greg getting miffed Tim smiling it all away
Finally we are in the car heading back down
The hill to Greg's house and to the rising
Jingoism of the 'news' that the chickens
Have come home to roost and by god some-
Thing's got to be done about it this is war
Man war good god yall what is it good for
You know the answer *absolutely* back in
Port Angeles proper it's back to more cnn
More information less answers more panic
Less certainty I call my friend John over in
Seattle and plan to go over the next day
Then it's back to the charade of everyday
Life croquet over at Greg's daughter's
House which used to be his mother's house
Lives encapsulated within the boundaries
Of this small town atop the country that was
Untouchable until a day ago Rockwell meets
Bosch what's wrong with this picture I can't
Seem to bring it all into perspective into
Focus as my friends romp and play plotting
And scheming to defeat each other on the
Battlefield of a lawn in northern WA I'm
Thinking my god what will become of us all
On the morning of my eighth day on the road
This really was a bad idea jumping around
All over the map like this never staying in
One spot very long anyway on this morning
Greg Colleen and I have a last oatmeal
Breakfast together the condemned man eats
A hearty meal before leaving the only town
He ever wanted to live in outside Los Angeles
Then Colleen leaves for work with a hug and
A don't be a stranger look and Greg and I
Pick up the granddaughter from school
I feel oddly estranged from these people
Not just because of the attacks but mostly
Because time has worked its magic on us

Roadkill

Whittling us down shadows of the past
This becomes a harbinger as most of my
Old acquaintances remain out of sync the
Past and present not melding together with
Any amount of ease not made easier by the
Brevity of my visit there just isn't enough
Time to redefine our commonality I tried to
Do too much I feel like such a fool the only
Saving grace is the attacks which block out
The awareness of this error in judgment as
I leave on the next leg of my trip Greg slips
Me some extra dough and I feel like I'm leaving
On a date in the family car there are so many
Unknowns right now he wants me to be extra
Careful we hug goodbye and I head down to
The street to check the oil and water get some
Gas on the way out of town the prices haven't
Gone through the roof yet everyone's nervous
That they might *we heard that some gas stations*
In KS were charging five bucks a gallon right
After the shit came down but that was quickly
Squelched by the boys in DC soon I'm heading
East past Sequim where a stretch of 101 is
Dedicated in loving memory to Jerry Garcia
Then it's past the Port Townsend turnoff
Towards the Hood Canal Bridge praying there
Aren't any nuclear subs running up the canal
Their slender black conning towers slicing
Through the water like the dorsal fins of orca
Pods I had previously seen up in the straits
With npr reports from a used to be all jazz
Station out of Tacoma I head towards Seattle
Taking the long way since the ferries are
Running slow what with every square inch
Of cargo space on each car being searched
Not that I have any contraband to worry about
I just don't want the hassle just want something
As normal as trees whizzing by and a clear
Sky devoid of jet contrails overhead like Adam
Must have felt after Eve and that damned snake
Cocked it all up I just wanted to go back to
The blissful state of ignorance of the before
time western WA state as far as I know is
a series of small towns connected by roads

Roadkill

And highways it is not subject to urban sprawl
Like CA except in a few places like Tacoma or
Seattle my next destination but Seattle is
Separated from Port Angeles by 100 miles of
Woodlands carefully manicured by the logging
Industry I make the run from PA to Sea-Tac
In under 3 hours and I don't even break 70mph
Even the dreaded Seattle traffic jams don't
Phase me I've heard stories about road rage
Up here and compared to LA these drivers
Are pathetic whining bastards who wouldn't
Survive a typical LA rush hour but I must
Remember that the poor Seattlites should
Be pitied inexperienced as they are though
Truth be told many of them are recovering
Angelinos immigrated here during the great
Land boom of the 80s you'd think they'd still
Remember how to drive evidently not so as
Usual I arrive early at John's house near the
U-Dub district it's hot in the car so I sit on
The wall in front of his house which is different
Than I remember it being it has been 14 years
Since I was last here it was cold and raining
As I recall there was ice on the ground the
Next morning not so now it's warm enough
That I wish I could put on my shorts down
The street comes a man jogging he is heavy
Though not as heavy as I but he wears only
A pair of skimpy black running shorts the
Sweat glistens on his skin as he nears me
The traffic on I-5 sounds like a seashore in
The distance a crow caw caw caws over-
Head I am aware of the passage of time
The beating of my heart I can picture it
Now as if I was sitting beside myself look-
Ing on observing myself this isn't something
I'm doing because of the recent events—
I always feel this kind of disconnection –but
It's more accented underscored as it were
By these events again I am observing dis-
Passionately as if this movie meant nothing
And everything to me just another fine fall
Day where even the locals confess to guilt
Over the balmy weather where elsewhere

Roadkill

Others are devastated under the same fall
Sunlight as if we should all suffer something
During this calamity even if only bad weather
I hope she doesn't get her wish *we ain't out
Of the woods yet* just in time John shows up
And we settle into that shorthand search
For the common ground knowing there isn't
Going to be much time to kibbitz John's wife
Chris shows up with his daughter and grand-
Daughter in tow the granddaughter is one year
Older than their daughter (must be the new
Math) then it's time for a quick snack and
We're off to drop the girls at dance class
*All girls must dance in the pacific north
West* John and I tour around Fremont a
Fledgling dot com center now gone bust
We run into a former student named
Chris who manages a bar nearby and much
To my surprise he's all grown up of course
 I haven't seen him in fourteen years but
Memory misfires occasionally so what can
You do wish I could talk to his mom she
Got me through some rough times when I
First quit drinking back in eighty-four so
I ask where she is now in Oakland he says
(mental note to call her when I get down
There) John and I head back home weird
Concept home I'm not anywhere close to
It but the surrogate model seems to work
Just fine later that evening I am surprised
Again when I meet old friend Jan and her
Mother as they join us for dinner more
Salmon (is that all they eat up here) very
Tasty I feel very strange around Jan but it
Is my own damn fault our history is twined
Around a common theme a school we three
Worked at for nearly a decade yet it was some
Twenty years back and though we try to stay
In touch we both suffered collateral damage
In the days that precipitated her move up here
That bumper car-roller coaster-tornado ride
Lasted longer than I care to remember so we
Stumble through the social graces but it is
Agreed that I will visit her on my way out of

Roadkill

Town when I head south again a visit as it turns
Out that is more telling about things past than
Things present as if the present is nothing more
Than a façade made up of the events of the past
As if I cannot escape my past because it's all that
I am and I suppose for my friends that I haven't
Seen in years it may be true since they have
Only their last memory of me to go by but even
My understanding of this limitation of their vision
Doesn't help to ease the frustration I feel since
I am so much more than I was at last sighting
Still one cannot escape the past at least not
Without altering one's identity our common
Past that little school in Manhattan Beach
Where so many kids and adults lives were
Changed including our own coinciding with
My years of darkness lost in the woods
Straying from the path I'm ready to have
The mother of all emotional-baggage
Garage sales *time to use it or lose it*
Day nine finds me studying raw footage
As if in deciphering it some new message
Some code might be cracked and some
Formula would produce a suitable
Answer $X + Y = $ *this* but nothing adds
Up to *no survivors* in the wreckage
And no bodies only parts and nothing
Equals the stunned faces of those working
At ground zero it is horrendous
I am not alone in a search for the formula
To explain this away I watch as the govt
Puts on its show of force our president
His game face a grim mask of determination
Of *we're gonna find the bastards who did
This* (where I wonder in the rubble mixed in
With the five thousand others who lost
Their lives in a flash) *and we're gonna
Make them pay* but before we can do
That we need all of you (the U in USA)
To get back out there and start to put
America back on her feet again buy
Baby buy with that the home shopping
Network went back on the air so the You
Of YouSA could start to heal itself back

Roadkill

To the regularly scheduled life folks
Nothing more to see right now
We'll keep you posted please let us do
Our jobs we've got a lot to figure out
Like how'd this happen and who all we can
Blame this on and it pretty much looks
Like this cat in Afghanistan this Osama
Bin Laden is the guy we're gonna pin
This on and if they don't give him over
To us well we'll just unleash the hounds
Of war on him and get medieval on his ass
We can do that now because we're on
Guard now and all the smart nations are
Behind us saying *go getum tiger* and the
Congress and the American people *who
Have been polled repeatedly and are
Fully in front of the Prez ready to drop
Their socks and grab their weapons to
Take this battle home* (no matter if home
Is some bombed out war torn country in
The middle east it don't matter boss man
Whatever it takes we're with you) we are
The You in USA
I worry about what this means to those
Pockets of resistance that I know are all
Over this country not to mention all those
Splinter groups who'd like nothing better
Than to get this country whipped up
And ambush it in the name of freedom
And their god-given rights all that blah
Blah so I got up and I drove around
While everyone was at work and none
Of the bookstores I visited were buying
My books making me think that this wasn't
A very patriotic town after all try and fail
To find several old pals from the dark days
But memory fails me and addresses are
Lost or they just don't want to be seen
With me in public or private *time heals
Nothing* now and why should it we've
Just been knocked down by a bunch of
Guys who lived here for years who lived
Off their hatred of us the US of A before
They caught their flights to heaven so why

Roadkill

Should it be different for lost friendships
Day ten finds me again in front of the TV
It's a day of national grieving and the
Govt has put on quite a show what with
Beautiful and heartrending songs to
Stir our national pride Denyse Price sings
America the Beautiful in the National
Cathedral in Washington DC and I know
I'm not the only one with goose bumps
As I prepare to head south today this
Being the day I also swing by Jan's
Place in South Seattle to dig on her digs
Later while I'm on the road southbound
A moment of silence is observed for the
Dead and I think that everything must
Surely stop for that moment (no dice)
Jan's loft is located in a warehouse
That's been condoed out her place
Going for a cool ninety-five thou and
Smartly outfitted to accommodate her
Newly found artistry and her practice
(She being an old school psych gal)
working the Jungian Cycle *no angles*
Please and making a comfy life in the
Process good for you Jan over tea and
Crumpets (yes) we catch up on 14 years
It's an outline of a chunk of living really
She doesn't have more than an hour to
Spare me not nearly enough to find
A commonality mostly we exchange
Pleasantries about the view and the
Noise and the artists in the building
All too soon I'm back on the I-5 heading
South back towards Portland and Leno
Beyond
Somewhere near the outskirts of
Downtown Portland I realize that this
Schedule I've set for myself is bullshit
All bets are off Rainy the schedule is
Out the window with the bath water
Baby and all near and dear what
Led up to that was I didn't have a
Map of Oregon except in my head
And I thought I knew where it was

Roadkill

(Over the river) so I just drove until
I crossed a river and started looking
For a downtown you see I had to
Drop off an order to Powell's Books
In downtown Portland I was on a
Small press mission doing my part
To get the country back up on its
Feet when I didn't find one I got off
And began searching I made a
Wide loop figuring to run into the
River and follow it boom or bust
My route took me through tweeker
Suburbs industrial wastelands (if
You need to dump something
This might be the place) passed
Road crews and more highway
Rehabilitation and when I hit
The freeway knew I'd screwed up
Bought a map from a guy with
An accent so thick I couldn't
Trust his directions and armed
With that and a cold iced tea I
Realized there were *two* rivers
And that's where I started to think
About what was going on this was
Not fun this was work this was
A fucking job I was just going
Through the motions of it I
Wasn't on vacation anymore (
Hell I wasn't even on a busman's
Holiday) I was losing interest in
Getting to Powell's I was sure I
Could mail it soon enough but
Then the second river appeared
And this was a Portland I recalled
From a trip back when I trusted
Someone more than I should
Have before I knew it I was driving
Down Burnside looking for 10th
Missed it do to some highway
Rehabilitation so circled back
(I was getting good at circling)
to find parking downtown Port
Land is a maze of oneway streets

Roadkill

And parking meters the meters
Gave you from five minutes to
Three hours to leave your car
Unattended the three hour zone
Was about ten blocks from Powell's
I just didn't feel like lugging my
Delivery that far after my third pass
Powell's was just a reflection in
My rear view mirror and after forty
Minutes in traffic so was Portland
Screw this
Somewhere near Scio *grass seed*
Capitol of the world I pull into a rest
Stop stretch the legs and see the
Sights while I'm sitting in my car
Eating a snack the welcome wagon
Shows up a trailer towed by an old
It's not that old pickup maybe 70s
Been rode hard and put away wet
Out of which come three big humans
You can hear the springs on the
Pickup groan in relief as they step
Out one of the gals must be pushing
Three hundred pounds quick as a lick
They get the thing set up well quick
As you can go being LARGE some
One is firing up the coffee while
The first customers are lining up
A radio clicks on and a man leans
In to hear better one of the three a
Man of some girth brings two jack
Stands to the rear of the trailer
Next he's got a bottle jack and
Some blocks of wood and I know
There's going to be trouble here
Because this has gotten Murphy's
Law written all over it he starts to
Jack it up but he didn't place the
Jack well and after about two inches
It pops out this brings the 300 pound
Gal out to investigate which raises the
Trailer a good three inches up which
Gives him enough room to work in
And soon the trailer is solid and level

Roadkill

I casually look around at the slow
Parade *numb parade as Scott Gordon
Calls it* of travelers slouches by can I
Be the only one watching this tableau
Of American the only war these folks
Are fighting is the war of exhaustion
No one seems to find this remotely
Interesting but me when I turn back
There is a man in snakeskin boots
And a rodeo belt buckle that could
Be dangerous asking directions to
Coos Bay *some kinda festival* he
Leaves with coffee in an old Cadillac

I follow his lead the sky is the color
Of lead I think that rain is coming
But I'm just a city boy right and
As Eugene looms ahead a few fat
Drops smear the dust around on
My windshield just enough to make
It interesting soon I'm driving slow
Down Springfield streets the trees
Chattering before the coming storm
I'm taking memory hits off this Davis
In 72 Reseda in 58 the streets are
Filled with gangs of roving leaves
There is an ominous heaviness in
The air the barometer is falling a
Breeze flutters the flags that have
Exploded over the country like spring
Wildflowers popping up everywhere
The national fever spreads like long
Shadows two fingers of darkness
Reach toward the west coast
Leno and his brother Bill and

Roadkill

Marjorie (mother) and I enjoyed a
Good meal the conversation flowing
Easily like it does between old friends
Or at least how it should later we sit
Outside enjoying the relative cool of
The evening but the air is heavy and
Thick I remark it feels like rain and
Sure enough fat drops begin to plop
Plop plop around us unlike the tropical
Rain I'm used to down south this
Storm brings thunder and lightning
With it which lasts long into the night
(Thank god for my earplugs) Leno reads
Me some favorite poesy by others and
Allows me to record him reading at several
Points during which crashing thunder
Punctuates his words at one rather
Poignant moment the curtain of thunder
Ceases and a train whistle rolls across
The landscape distant and ghostly the hairs
On the back of my neck go up mostly
Because a bolt of lightening strikes down
The street but also because for just a moment
A beautiful sense of "uhuh" filled the room
Leno and I get along so easily you would
Think we'd known each other for ever and
Perhaps it's true if it could happen the
Same way with Todd Moore and I then
Why not Leno and I we discuss plans
For tomorrow there's some sort of parade
In downtown Eugene in the morning
Marjorie plans on going we do not we
Plan instead to go to Tsunami Books
Near the hardware store Leno thinks
I might be able to sell some books
They always buy mine he tells me
The lightning continues it strobes
Outside the window next to my sofa bed
A giant candle flickering in the dark
Trees disappearing and reappearing
Beautiful but scary I closed my eyes and
Prayed for NY and sleep in the morning Bill
Marjorie headed out while Leno and I got
Our act together outside the sky is gray

Roadkill

Foreboding in spite of the fact that the
Storm has so obviously moved on the
Neighborhood is very quiet no sound
No barking dogs no cars nothing seems
To be awake yet and it's nearly nine o'clock
I'm surprised Leno assures me that this is
Life in a small town nothing special about
It we head out to the hardware store (I tell
Him I can replace a bad switch in his bed
Room before I leave) Leno wants me to
Stay longer but I must get back to my bro's
Because he was in near hysterics when I
Called him last night the 9-11 horror had
Knocked him for a loop I never had heard
Him talking so crazy so I planned on leaving
As early as possible because it would be
A long long drive over five hundred miles
Forcing me to drive for nearly eight and
A half hours through mountainous terrain
Over passes that divide CA from ORE down
The I-5 past mount Shasta and nearby Redding
People I would have visited there but now all
That is changed and I just wanna get to home
Sweet home where I might get a good nights
Rest (I'm averaging three to four now – I'm
Gonna need a vacation to recover from this
When I do get back) maybe I can find some
Excuse to make the drive I won't be flying any
Time soon it would be nice to be able to layover
In Redding would make the trip bearable *funny*
I used to love to drive long hours on the road
Meant nothing to me to be driving six eight
Ten hours now I'd rather be walking around
Or sitting in some room finding the common
Ground there must be someone on the Lummox
Roster who lives up here who'd put me up
And up with me maybe my on again off again
Friend Sam who still owes me a ladder but that's
Another story
I-5 drops down through WA OR and the long run
Through CA until it slams into the Mexican border
On the map it is a red line slightly thicker than the
One or one-ninety-nine but equal to the one-oh-one
Or the ninety-nine it appears to be a by-pass free

Roadkill

Way as are many of our modern superhighways
It's ironic that our supposed love affair with
The car has led us to adopt this soulless byway
For the part between points A and B the part
Where most of the journey exists yet little of the
Sight seeing occurs the I-5 from Portland south
Is a steadily evolving pastoral an ode to the
Color brown so that when you reach Red Bluff
You are down with the brown: the dirt of the land
The grasslands the trees the occasional farm
House the dogs the kids the dirty brown hills
To the east farmland as far as the eye can tell
It stays that way until you reach the I-80 near
Fairfield nearly as long as OR is wide but I
State my case too unequivocally there are
Many interesting stretches of super-highway
Including the trip from Grant's Pass to Redding
A two hundred mile run that takes you up
Over the knuckle mountains south of Medford
Down through mesas and volcanic cinder
Cones I saw a perfect one rising in the distance
It may have been Mount Ashland but at
First I thought it was Mt. Shasta (but
Shasta's an older more eroded structure)
The volcano was a sort of geologic loner
Set off by itself on a plane of recent (what's
Recent to a volcanic cinder cone) lava flows
And basaltic events not to mention a good
Scouring by some ancient glacier so on
Into upstate CA tundra towns like
Yreka and Weed and the heavily antiqued
And forested Dunsmuir named after
John Muir somehow took a little side trip
Through Dunsmuir just to see what I
Was by-passing it was a sleepy looking
Affair under gray wet skies more shades of
Brown even though the forest surrounded
The town the sky was a strange shade of
Blue steel and here and there tufts of fog
In big fluffy patches clung to stands of
Pine and fir trees as if torn loose from
Low slung rain-laden clouds that had just
Passed overhead it was footstamping cold
In Dunsmuir and I wasn't even half way

Roadkill

There yet and yet it was good to be
Distracted finally from the horrors man-
Made of recent days gone by rest of drive
Uneventful except for miles and miles of
Early fall dead grasses stretching away
From either shoulder dusty brown blur
Concealing towns like Corning Orland
Willows Artois Delevan Dunnigan and
Arbuckle where I stopped for gas the sun
Casting long dusty shadows the gas
Pumps working overtime to fill ATVs
RVs and other off-roaders heading for
Clear Lake (maybe) to the west this is the
Eye-five most know from here south
To Bakersfield as that thoroughfare
Of monotonous speed and destination
Nearly get lost in the dark drive south
On five-oh-five which short cuts to the
West on eye-eighty the last leg before
East Bay and SF beyond but I hit red
Lights before I get as far as Rockville
And in my stubborn impatience to
JUST GET THERE I jump on the twelve
And head for Napa thinking in my
Fuzzy way that it is near San Rafael
Of course it's not but I hopscotch my
Way through the dark empty spaces
In the undeveloped (for now) fields
Between Ignacio and Sonoma to
The one-oh-one south (blessed relief)
To San Rafael lit up for annual film fest
(No sign of bombscares here) my
Bro fully recovered from phone call
In Eugene night before – business
As usual now – except no tennis matches
To occupy our time together watched
Instead "normal" programming for first
Time in nearly a week shows I was un
Familiar with: The Man Show – pure
Chauvinism – embarrassing in all it's
Soft core psuedo-entertainment and
The sopranos – t & a mafia show – and I
Began to think about what might make
Bin Laden and his fanatic ilk hate us

Roadkill

So bitterly all this trivial crap served
Up to the American public in the
Name of God and Country and the
All mighty dollar and for a brief moment
During the cheerleaders on trampolines
Segment at the end of the Man Show I
Thought MY GOD maybe those muslim
Terrorists are right maybe WE are the
Great SATAN after all later on MSNBC
I watched 24 Hours At Ground Zero and
Knew that no matter how evil the big
Corps were or how greedy as a country
We might be we still deserved BETTER
Than we got
But it is always the few who benefit
From the efforts of the many always the
Most with the least who get the screws
Whether it be from the govt or some
Rich bastards telling us (both the Us in
USA and the us in all countries) the
Working poor even the middle class
Though I haven't been in that class for
Many many years – since my youth
The Bushes and Bin Ladens will always
Get their kicks from the common folk
Both have God on their side (our God's
Gonna kick your God's ass) pick your
God and place your bets
Bend over and kiss your ass goodbye
This ain't over yet – there's more
Surprises planned by our enemies
Say goodbye to your rights to humane
Treatment and say hello to the screws
To the six day work week and no
Health care and no education and no
Sound way to deal with the pandemics
Of aids and crack and rape and a
Flood of babies left to their own devices
Because we've got a war on terrorism
Here and there's no time to waste
Worrying about environments or oil
Or surpluses or deficits or condoms
Or blowing up some guy's mud hut
And his camel unless it's with a

Roadkill

Valuable two million dollar
Smart bomb (aw but what the heck
We didn't make them to just sit a
Round and collect dust did we)
It's all right ma I'm only
Cryin'
Next day hooked up with Carol she
Of the longtime back days just past
My seventeenth year the crazy days
Of youth and the mad rush of hippies
And manic creation psychedelic
Experimentation halcyon days buried
But not quite forgotten she married a
Guy named Carroll (yeah Carol Carroll)
Who bore a striking resemblance to
Bin Laden except he was two years
Gone from this world – died during
My last visit up here in ninety-nine
Also the last time I saw Carol – and
A guy who couldn't keep his dick in
His pants to save his soul we talked
For a long while in her tiny two-room
Apartment (used to be a brothel) in
San Rafael's downtown catering to
Artists mostly studios with a community
Bathroom and cheap rent (like a dorm
She tells me with good light) she tells me
About her tumor even had a catscan
Picture of it just had it removed as
Big as a navel orange wrapped around
Her optic nerve and carotid artery
Silently growing inside her head since
Reagan was in office now she waits
For her brain to re-occupy that fist
Sized space in her skull praying that
Nothing breaks during the move it's
A slow process later we get coffee
And a roll and continue what is turning
Out to be our longest conversation ever
I like Carol we come from similar lives
She's one of the few people I know
From my good old bad old days who
I still can talk to most everyone else
Has returned to the roots of their up

Roadkill

Bringing we have much in common
Next day I'm backtracking my route
Driving to Sonoma to visit former San
Pedro homey Sandro who just published
His first novel about growing up in the
Flats back in the day Sandro and mujer
Live at the end of this dusty road outside
Town in a concrete box that was dropped
Into a field like a piece of skylab or the
Mere space station very bohemian very
Late nineties Bauhaus revivalist yet
Sandro is all smiles all six foot eight
Inches of him still toting the same back
Pack still talking all cocky still living
On the edge while his wife finishes a
Freelance editing job down in el lay
We drive into town and get breakfast
He tells me how it is in the publishing
World of agents and contracts and up
Front money (refers to his five-figure
Advance as chump change) and how his
Next book is gonna set everyone on
Their ear I listen politely thinking I
Wish I had his moxie or at least his
Cojones which must be huge later
We go to Readers Books where I do
My little pitch and leave off a few books
Hoping to return later to check stock
Driving out of Sonoma back to bro's
House then on to JB's house in East
Bay I get off the freeway above Berkeley
And cruise gentle through old neighbor
Hoods where as a young man I first
Flirted with this lifestyle where I first
Got into trouble (I pulled on trouble's
Braids) passed the old haunts as
Near as I could remember didn't stop
The car and walk around didn't want
To think I've put those sad memories
Behind me but still can recall heady
Moments spent in the arms of Karen
Coupled with the surgical accuracy of
Love's twisting knife afterwards so my
Quest to resolve to forget and forgive

Roadkill

Or however that goes each time I'm
Near there I always try to purge a
Little more now it's to the point that
Berkeley is just another town where
The rent is too high and the streets
Are too crowded on the radio KPFA
I listen to the opinions of Afghanis
About the pending war in their country
Granted most interviewed spoke freely
So I imagine they are inclined towards
The Taliban ideal but most agreed that
It wasn't the fault of the Afghan people
That the US was attacked and they
Shouldn't be punished for this – I
Agreed with this until the interviewer
Suggested that this was why the
Americans are held in such high
Contempt around the world because
We are always trying to blow/buy off
Our enemies – there you go again
Confusing the us with US it's
Wrong to blame the many for the
Actions of the few if you do it
Selectively I mean I don't like it
When we as citizens do it or when
Our war mongering govt does it or
Some other war mongering govt does
It or even when everyone is jumping
On the bad guy bandwagon what are
We animals chest thumping animals
Marking our territory by pissing on
Our neighbors aren't we better than
That how are we going to fight a war
On terrorism when we have terrorists
Living right here in America and I don't
Mean Arab moles planted here by Al
Queda either I mean guys like Ted
Kasinski the CIA and the state of Idaho
Are we going to root out and expunge
All sources of terrorism and all the
States who provide safehaven what
About Isreal South Africa France Ireland
To name a few where will the US/us draw
The line I want us/US to stop and think

Roadkill

Before we act out I know someone's
Going to get a whipping but I don't know
How the great Bush is going to decide
He certainly has a lot of people at work
Helping him decide why in just the past
Week the FBI has compiled a huge list
Of conspirators and is hot on the money
Trail tracing the footsteps of the nineteen
Bastards who actually did this to us/US
Back to bin Lauden's smug little rich mug
Because we have to have evidence to
Present to the court of world opinion
To justify our bombing Afghanistan back
To the stoneage (a handful of rocks tossed
Across the border from Pakistan would
Suffice) yeah it's gotta be done legal
Signed sealed delivered
Lookout ma I'm only dyin'
The eastbay is a swirl of activity as we
Prepare to do our bit for the boys and
Girls over there I stop at a market just
Over the Oakland border to get some
Grub – a loaf of bread some apples and
Some celery – nine bucks nine lousy
Dollars for three things the other
Shoppers around me seem almost
Giddy as if someone was handing out
Free samples of the blood of Kali –
One sip and you're hooked one sip
And whatever the bossman tells
You to do you do it gladly because
Everyone wants to be a happy
Camper right out in the parking lot
I make up a PB& H sandwich and
Muse about things I've seen lately
Besides that damned tower pulling
Jets into it like some GD magnet
Watching my bro do his best
Impression of me twenty years back
With glazed eyes and face awash
In the flickering colors from the tv
Carol and some newbie AA guy
Having an animated conversation
Where nothing of substance is said

Roadkill

And no information is passed except
For the secret AA code of innuendo
And suggestive facial movements
Greg handing me some extra dough
"Just in case" money suddenly I'm
Lower than a snake's belt buckle so it's
Off to Lake Merit for some killing time
JB won't be home from work for some
Time yet and her snookums gets insane
After about thirty minutes of me being
Around JB and I go back over ten years
But her hubs and I well we just never
Got it right from the beginning so I
Spend my time wondering what he'll
Come up with next he's the jock I never
Had but JB loves him and I love her
So I take it as it comes and try to leave
With some dignity he's a real lucky guy
Like the old saying goes "you don't
Miss your water 'til the well runs dry"
I make a foray over to SF but it is a
Disaster no parking where I need to go
I miss my connection too many people
The whole fucking town is crazy with
People and cars it's much worse than
I remember it being two short years ago
Don't know how these people do it
How do they live here Christ the rent
Alone would be incentive enough to
Move out to the country and paint
Your mailbox blue imagine when I
Lived here my share of the rent was
Never more than fifty bucks you people
Are nuts so I blow off SF and head
"Home" knowing that next day I'll
Be back here to meet with poet Allan
D Winans briefly then off to Santa Cruz
Only a few more days of this and I'll
Be pulling into my parking spot behind
My building on fourth street glad that it's
Over but sorry to see it end (wish I had
A river I could sail away on) just thinking
Of Leonard J. Cirino's book The Terrible
Wilderness of Self thinking that this

Roadkill

Wilderness is not so terrible not nearly
As terrible as the world of humans
Bustling around in each other's business
Blindly killing off species after species
Without even knowing it without even
Caring ignorant and insensitive to the
Harsh beauty of each day on this rock

As we spin through on our way to some
Finite grace some simple patch of under
Standing some ready to wear nirvana it's
Not the people so much as the lonely
Spots on the road that I crave the way
An old fence might struggle up the side
Of a hill or the way a cloud stands out in a
Storm as if it's taking a solo the way
The sea looks off of Point Sur like molten
Lead curling in from its trans-Pacific
Journey the way hiway one seems to
Steer clear of the effects of man's
Occupation of this rugged terrain this
Western rim of the continent the way
It passes through all the little burgs
From Half Moon Bay Santa Cruz with
That strange fallen lighthouse just
North of town all the way down through
Carmel Big Sur Lucia Gorda San Simeon
Cambria Harmony Cayucos Morro Bay
Before hopping inland again to San Luis
Obispo all of this incessant speed in
Search of what
What
The perfect stretch of road

Roadkill

Somewhere south of Big Sur I will find
That perfect stretch more a perfect sense
Of what makes for the definitive the
Essence of ROAD where all the parts come
Together to add up to the WHOLE is it
The journey the overview of adventures
The routes taken or not the movement
From point A to B the people that one
Meets along the way (both new and old
Friends) or is there more
For me there is a rhythm that one
Settles into a kind of meditation of move
Ment I've always associated this with
The three by six inch rectangle of contact
Where the rubber hits the road but it
May also apply to flight or other forms
Of travel (imagine what it would be
Like to traverse [any] continent by
Foot or horseback) I only know this
Rhythm from the many car/truck travels
I have made in my lifetime opportunities
For movement not only from without but
From within where the grandeur of
Some image be it stony crag or sweeping
Coastline of mighty redwood or miniscule
Wildflower of swooping bird or bounding
Deer whatever it is that catches you up and
Makes you pause and wonder at your own
Place in all this are you merely here to
Witness this moment and record it or is
There perhaps a greater part in this
Tragi-comedy for you some moment
In this dance of electrons that you almost
Understand some thing you almost see
You can call it navel-gazing or whatever

Roadkill

You like lord knows it certainly isn't the
Fashion these days to look within for
The answer no it's all about the action
Let's roll let's get it done let's kick some
Ass xenophobia be damned it's time to
Step up to the plate and take a swing
For god and country step right up it's
Only two for a dollar knock the turban
Off the arab and win a prize make your
Country proud son let's all do our part
To bring truth justice and the American
Business plan to all who cry out for help
This is war baby let our enemies know
The wrath of our go[l]d a god who moves
With stealth and righteous indignation
(And the blessings of enron and gm)
You can't tell the terrorists from the free
Dom fighters well just look harder and
Wait for the govt to point them out
I drove 2900 miles to find that perfect
Stretch of road found it just south of
The Henry Miller Library where all
Elements came together and for a
Minute or two I couldn't tell you who
Was driving whom on the route of one
Der alone except for the occasional
Car or light truck with your thoughts
Fading in and out back and forth be
Tween demands of driving like this:
Check the rear view check the front view
Think watch the road watch the curves
Don't take this turn too fast think
Change the music Think check the
Gauges look at that line of fence
Snaking up the ridge look at the
Ocean think it looks like molten lead
Check the rear view wonder why
That guy is tailgating me WHY would
Anyone be in such a hurry on this
Two lane check time think about
9-11 is that the sun breaking through
Calculate gas mileage watch for a
Turnout let the asshole meet his
Destiny that much sooner on and on

Roadkill

Like that juggling the moment with
The process the here and now with
The then and there it's a dance a
Partnership between driver and
Machine with a pockmarked
Stretch of asphalt for a dance floor
And the lonesome mid-coast of
California on this day draped in
Shades of gray and muted greens
Serving as the dance hall
Only a few days out of LA now waiting
In Eats on Clement Street in SF for
A breakfast rendezvous with Al Winans
It's a gray drizzly day perhaps a typical
Day here in the city this café is warm
And pleasant the cappuccino is strong
And refreshingly bitter a TV drones in
The background I listen subconsciously
The mantra has not changed much since
9-11 body count updates have been
Replaced with body part count updates
Wall Street has reopened the country
Has breathed a sigh of relief and the
Cleanup at ground zero continues
Around the clock bin Ladden is the
Bad guy du jour and the prez wants
Everyone to get back to being good
Americans: traveling spending money
And going about our lives as if nothing
Had ever happened as if that's really
Possible maybe if we went on a nation
Wide drunk took a long weekend and
Got so plowed that we but no that
Wouldn't work no we'd need one of
Those mib memory erasers one click
And it's all forgotten just look over
Here Al shows up and we converse
While working on our omelets not
About the current shit which I'm
Glad of so tired of those images
From only a week ago those
Images branded on my eyeballs
No instead we talk about poets
Petty squabbles and feuds it is a

Roadkill

Conversation that seems inane now
Back in LA it will seem more important
But right now I feel suddenly chilled
As if a shadow had been cast over me
A shadow that has been creeping this
Way from the east for a week now
I think of that rose colored moon the
First night of my journey disappearing
Into the gray clouds overhead just as
Manhattan disappeared into a gray
Cloud and now under a gray sky in
SF and I feel an emptiness in my belly
And must excuse myself to hit the can
For fear that the espresso was kicking in
Early a little cold water in the face and
The feeling passes I sit back down Al
Picks up where he left off until it's
Time for me to leave next stop Santa
Cruz I consider hitting a few book
Joints but decide I just want to get
This over next thing I know I'm driving
Past Marc Olmstead's house on my way
To highway one-o-one which passes
Near Golden Gate Park – I marched
There once in an anti-war rally in 69 or 70
Nobody remembers those days now but
Maybe in days to come we will remember
Bringing back a public conscience and I
Don't mean the so-called anarchist move
Ment either – then it's south through SF
And down to Half Moon Bay perhaps the
Beginnings of the wild coast as Judson
Crews called it his wc actually starting
Just south of Monterey so I take some
Poetic license I listen to radio npr
Mostly these days listen to the chattering
Voices still trying to make sense out
Of all this still trying to point out the
Who what where and when of it all
When I hear someone say tears are the
Same color no matter who cries them
It must be time to take a little break so
I pull off the road near San Gregario
Make a PB&H stretch my legs check out

Roadkill

The surf and take a little walk the beach
Is narrow I can't tell if the tide is coming
Or going I make it a short walk take a pee
And head back come up to the parking
Area to the north and as I'm walking
Along I come to a low gully with a narrow
Pathway at the foot of this path I can see
The remains of some recent rendezvous
Empty 40s a winebottle some food wrappers
And I'm certain if I ventured into this
Thicket of secrets I'd find other trash of a
More intimate kind I think I must be getting
Old to pass up a chance to go exploring
Like this all the times in the past I would
Pick through the debris left behind by
Others especially when it came to man's
Second favorite pastime: sneaking around
Doing something wrong number one being
Trying to get away with something by
Pulling the wool over someone else's eyes
All the other secret spots I'd known began
To float to the surface of my memory in
My youth I had done my fair share of
Skulkage seeking out some little sleepy
Hollow or no-tel motel to take care of my
Business under the cover of leafy bough or
Cottage cheese ceiling later I grew out
Of it some never do though addicted to
The life the adrenaline rush of living
On the edge over two wheels over it
Which is the way I feel right now but I'm
Heading for Santa Cruz to meet the last
Two poets before I head into SoCal –
Will Taylor Jr and Brian Morrisey of
Poesy magazine so I shake it off and
Pull back onto route one heading south
Outside Santa Cruz where the one
Pushes up over the bluffs/cliff line
There are the remains of a building
I've heard a story of an old lighthouse
That fell into the sea and this might
Be all that remains a startling image
But one of the reasons I look forward
To this drive peppered as it is with

Roadkill

These surprises it's what makes route
One-der stand out there's something
About the immediacy of the scenery
It's close proximity it's suddenness
It's so personal partly due to the
Fact that route one is so windy
That you can't possibly drive faster
Than forty mph in most sections (
The last few miles into SC are proof
You can't drive faster than ten mph
Since the road is all torn up *water*
Main upgrade June 01 to Aug 01
Typical county/state job always behind
Schedule) once in town I'm just
Cruising around killing time before
Heading over to Will's apt which I
Suddenly realize I don't have the
Address for but miraculously I
Remember where it is from when
I was there last in 99 cruising
Through town I begin to feel uneasy
As if being on the open road
With it's vast expanses and vistas
And anonymity the sheer significance
Of being out there out there beyond
The fences the town limits as if all
This has made me ill-at-ease around
Crowds or traffic though cars seem less
Threatening I will wend my way through
These crowded streets back to Will's
Crowded house where we gather to
Share poesy over fondue and cocktails
I forego both in favor of NA beer and
A tuna sandwich Will and Brian are
Young lions here in the blossoming
SC poetry scene while I'm some funky
Old guy a little whacked out from
Whiteline fever I remember sitting
On Will's couch with my little video
Camera in my lap thinking I've been
Doing this forever this going into someone's
Home and recording them in their nest
Reading their shit or going to someplace
To read to a bunch of strangers I've been

Roadkill

Doing this for years and years and YEARS
But the truth is both Will and Brian have
Been at this longer than I by at least two
Or three years they're my seniors yet
They treat me as an equal amazing and
With aplomb another poet is contacted
And she brings her husband who is
Bristling with ideas about how to
Prevent another 9-11 arm all the
Passengers with 9mm's is the most
Bizarre one yet it makes some
Small sense so we all nod in concession
Almost too shellshocked to have an
Independent thought in our heads not
Soon enough he leaves for the safety of
His home *his home* I am envious though
Glad I'm not living with all that she
Reads some of her poems which are
Okay but since 9-11 things that are okay
Just aren't good enough any more and
Okay poetry just doesn't get it done for
Me anymore maybe once that asbestos-
Leaden dust settles and we're back to
Business as usual maybe then okay
Will be acceptable again eventually
I beg off and hit the hay (in this case
Four seat cushions from a sofa laid
Out on the floor is my mattress) will
Get up early as usual and head
South past Monterey and Big Sur
Down highway one meantime I
Must get some sleep thank god
For my earplugs as Will and his
Guests continue to party late
Into the night no one will greet
Me in the morning not even after I
Shower so I jot down my thanks
On a piece of paper and hop on
The freeway to join the rest of the
Commuters (another parking lot)
Heading for Monterey or Salinas to
The south after nearly getting
Sideswiped by a silver SUV I realize
I'm getting a little loopy from being

Roadkill

On the road a little too long sleeping
On floors sofas the occasional bed
In so many foreign houses so many
Strangers who seem like friends
So many friends who have become
Strangers and I think it's good that
Should I decide to do it I could be home
tonight somewhere between Pacific Grove
And Monterey I remember that on one of
My youthful swings across the state hitch
Hiking I witnessed an amazing lightshow
In the sky above this road (of course back
Then there was nobody around little traffic
And none of the malling of the landscape)
A missile was fired from Vandenburg and
As it left the atmosphere right overhead the
It looked like a milk thistle and an umbrella
Opening and then it was gone vanished
Someone made the sound of a cork popping
We all laughed and got back into the car
Today however you couldn't see an el-ten-
Eleven overhead unless it was making
A final run on the Monterey Aquarium
The marine layer so thick and damp
Hovering low above Carmel as if in
Sympathy for the thick gray cloud
Hovering still over ground zero in NYC
By the time I get to Lucia the sun
Begins a valiant effort to come out
By San Simeon it is a successful
Effort and a beautiful California day
Is born crisp and radiant a day
That I savor the union between the
Road and my ride and I I'm finally
Seeing feeling it this is it baby
Full driving oneness my loopyness
Forcing me to pay really close
Attention to the countless gray
Images that drift or jolt into view
Forgotten images remembering
Instead sheer cliffs dizzying drops
And foggy curves this Brave Wild
Coast as Judson Crews called it
Home of Henry Miller and other

Roadkill

Crack pot poets of Eselen and
Hog Heaven Big Sur remains a
Mythic place Mecca for my mis-
Begotten youth a memory that
I only half remember the hippy
Highway route one-der but today
The sea is a flat pale green canvas
Peppered with dark brown splats of
Kelp and seaweed in some places
It's a fifty-fifty split of brown to sea
Green but here the kelp huddles
Between two outcroppings the sea
Mutters to itself but I haven't the
Heart to decipher it in the distance
A bird is laughing like a hyena
The sea begins to chortle as a set
Rolls in from Japan it is all so
Soothing that I almost slip into
A trance I am saved from my reverie
By an SUV which whizzes past me
On a late date in Cambria fog scrapes
Along the hillside pushed by a fresh
Breeze everything appears muted
Almost dumbed down like the whole
Country as the man in the east prepares
To hurl our might at a man further to the
East playing eenie meenie minnie moe
With cruise missiles and cave openings
Highway one moves like a ragged line
Over ancient bridges and around
Hairpin curves that force you to slow
Down and smell the brakes burning
This road forces you to reacquaint
Yourself with the *PROCESS* of driving
The *ACT* if you will it is not a rote
Exercise or a routine though most
People drive as if they were on a
Towline as if someone else was
Controlling traffic flow but here
On this two lane hairpin curved
Decrepit stretch of asphalt one
Cannot long ignore the slow
Sharp curve signs for long without
Dire consequences by the time I

Roadkill

Hit San Simeon the road has stretched
Out into a long low throw down the
Coast past Harmony Cayucos Morro
Bay and back onto the well lit here
Comes the sun highway one-oh-one
And before you know it I'm back home
Again shooting the breeze with my
Mates at Portfolio back among the
Company of people I know no longer
Racing from point A to point B ah
Home at last I can almost taste the
Air around the harbor that rancid blend
Of diesel Sulfur fish and crude oil
All these images are punched into my
head and ratcheted down tightly
around my soul and there they remain

3/11/02

APPENDIX –

NORTHERN ROUTE:
Long Beach to Los Angeles via seven-ten
And eye-five to Tujunga via the two
And two-ten west to Foothill Blvd to
The eye-five to Valencia to one-twenty-six
To Filmore to Santa Paula to Ventura and
One-oh-one to thirty-three and Ojai to
One-fifty back to one-oh-one and
Carpenteria Summerland Santa
Barbara Goleta Naples Gaviota Las
Cruces Buelton Los Alamos Santa Maria
Arroyo Grande Pismo Beach San Luis
Obispo Lucia Atascadero Paso Robles
Bradley San Ardo San Lucas King City
Greenfield Soledad Gonzales Chualar
Salinas Santa Rita Prunevale Gilroy
San Martin Morgan Hill Coyote Campbell
San Jose Cupertino via the two-eighty
West past Sunnyvale Mountain View
Los Altos Menlo Park Redwood City
San Mateo South San Francisco Daly City
San Francisco back onto the one-oh-one
Past Sausalito Mill Valley to San Rafael
Then north past Ignacio Navato Petaluma
El Verano Cotati Rohnert Park Roseland
Santa Rosa Larkfield Windsor Healdsburg
Lytton Geyserville Asti Cloverdale Preston
Hopland Ukiah Calpella Willits Longvale
Laytonville Cummings Leggett Richardson
Grove Garberville Phillipsville Miranda
Meyers Flat Weott Bridgeville Scotia Rio
Dell Alton Campton Heights Fortuna Loleta
Bayview Eureka Samoa Arcata Mckinleyville
Trinidad Orick Klamath Crescent City and east
On the one-ninety-nine past Gasquet O'Brien
Illinois Valley Cave Junction Kerby Selma
Wonder Wilderville to Grants Pass and

Roadkill

    Eye-five and on past Merlin Sunny Valley
    Wolf Creek Azalea Canyonville Myrtle Creek
    Winston Green Roseburg Winchester
    Wilbur Sutherlin Oakland Anlauf Curtin
    Cottage Grove Saginaw Walker Creswell
    Goshen Eugene then east on one-
    Twenty-six to Springfield then back to eye-
    Five and north past Coburg Rowland Albany
    Keizer/Salem Brooks Woodburn Hubbard
    Wilsonville then east around Portland on
    The two-oh-five Dulles Loop through Fairview
    And Orchards back to eye-five and Vancouver
    Woodland Kalama Carrols Kelso Ostrander
    Castle Rock Toledo Chehalis Centralia
    Fords Prairie Grand Mound Tumwater
    Olympia then west onto the one-oh-one
    Past Shelton and north past Skokomish
    Indian Rez Hoodsport Lilliwaup Eldon
    Brinnon Quilcane Leland Maynard and
    Gardiner then west past Blyn Sequim
    Agnew to Port Angeles

    SOUTHERN ROUTE:
    East on the one-oh-one back to
    Maynard then onto the one-oh-four to
    Shine and south past Lynwood on the
    three past Poulsbo Silverdale Chico
    Bremerton Port Orchard (Sixteen) Purdy
    Gig Harbor Tacoma to the eye-five north
    Past Milton Redondo Des Moines to Seattle
    Then retrace south on eye-five past Tacoma
    Puyallup Lakewood Center Du Pont Lacey
    Olympia and retrace eye-five south through
    Washington and Oregon all the way back
    To Grants Pass and continuing south on
    Eye-five past Rogue River Gold Hill Central
    Point Medford Phoenix Talent Ashland
    Klamath Falls Junction Siskiyou Colestin

Roadkill

Hilt Hornbrook Yreka Grenada Edgewood
Weed Mount Shasta Dunsmuir Castella
Lakehead O'brien Lake Shasta Project City
Enterprise Redding Anderson Cottonwood
Red Bluff Tehema Corning Orland Artois
Willows Delevan Maxwell Williams
Arbuckle Dunnigan then south on the
Five-oh-five past Madison Winters
Allendale to eye-eighty past Vacaville
Fairfield Rockville Vallejo to thirty-seven
West and one-oh-one junction at Ignacio
Then retrace one-oh-one south to San
Rafael then onto seventeen to Richmond
Past El Cerrito Albany Berkeley Piedmont
To Oakland then west past Emeryville to
Eye-eighty toll booths into San Francisco
To route one along the coast past Lake
Merced Broadmoor Edgemar Pacific Manor
Pacifica Vallemar Rockaway Beach Linda
Mar Pedro Valley Montara Moss Beach
El Granada Half Moon Bay San Gregorio
Pescadero Swanton Davenport Santa Cruz
Scotts Valley Soquel Aptos Moss Landing
Castroville Marina Seaside Pacific Grove
Del Ray Oaks Monterey Carmel Carmel Woods
Notleys Lodge Big Sur State Hot Springs Lucia
Gorda San Simeon Cambria Harmony
Cayucos Morro Bay Baywood Park
And Retrace from San Luis Obispo south on
The one-oh-one back to Long Beach and
Home

3247 miles round trip in sixteen days

ABOUT THE AUTHOR

RD Armstrong, a self styled Road Scholar, reluctant gypsy and vagabond, has spent many of his years on the "coast route", choosing, whenever possible, to get from point A to point B via car and/or truck. In the case of all three poems, the vehicle was an '88 Nissan Sentra.

Raindog, as he is known to his friends, is a man, driven. Not only does he seek the knowledge of things (the mechanics of how things work), but he also seeks to understand his purpose (if any) in the grand scheme of things. Raindog feels he has a calling to fulfill...he just can't seem to decipher what it is; and the gods are always busy when he turns to them for a clue.

He has labored in the trenches of the Alternative Small Press since 1996, both as editor/publisher of The Lummox Journal and as publisher of the Little Red Book series with nearly sixty titles by some of the ASP's best/least known poets. In the Lummox Journal's one hundred and twelve issues, he interviewed nearly one hundred poets, writers and artists, always with the emphasis on their creative process.

Although he has been writing off and on since 1968, his most prolific period began in 1993. Since then he has written poetry, short-fiction and essays. A collection of his best poems appears in Fire and Rain, a two volume set, published by Lummox Press.

RD Armstrong's books include PEDRO BLUE (Vinegar Hill Press), Paper Heart (Lummox Press), In Memoriam (The Inevitable Press), The San Pedro Poems (Lummox Press), RoadKill (12 Gauge Press), Last Call: the Legacy of Charles Bukowski and The Hunger (both by Lummox Press). His poems have been published in over one hundred small press magazines and in over sixty websites.

Visit www.lummoxpress.com for a complete picture of RD's empire.

www.ingramcontent.com/pod-product-compliance
Lightning Source LLC
Chambersburg PA
CBHW071314110426
42743CB00042B/1994